British Relations with Sind

1799-1843

British Relations with Sind

1799-1843

An Anatomy of Imperialism

ROBERT A. HUTTENBACK

University of California Press

Berkeley and Los Angeles

1962

UNIVERSITY OF CALIFORNIA PRESS
BERKELEY AND LOS ANGELES, CALIFORNIA

CAMBRIDGE UNIVERSITY PRESS
LONDON, ENGLAND

© 1962 BY THE REGENTS OF THE UNIVERSITY OF CALIFORNIA
LIBRARY OF CONGRESS CATALOG CARD NUMBER: 62-9266
DESIGNED BY THEO JUNG

To Freda

Preface

GENERATIONS of British schoolboys have learned about the characteristic but apocryphal telegram Sir Charles Napier supposedly sent to London after his defeat of the Amirs of Sind at Miani. "Peccavi," he punned—"I have sinned [Sind]." [1] The tale has linked, probably for all time, the name of Charles Napier and the conquest of the lower Indus Valley by the East India Company. Napier, however, is only the final, if possibly the most important, actor in the drama culminating in the annexation of Sind. The story begins long before his arrival on the scene, and he is concerned merely with the last act.

Throughout most of the eighteenth century the policies of the East India Company were governed largely by considerations of commerce and finance. Thus the Company maintained factories in Sind from 1635 to 1662 and from 1758 to 1775. In the latter year the establishments were removed because of internal unrest and the decline of textile manufactures formerly characterized as "the flower of the whole parcel and preferred before all others in their making." [2] But the act of 1784, which created the Board of Control for India, greatly increased the role of the British Government in the determination of Indian policy; thereafter British relations with Sind were governed by the broader considerations of national security and international affairs. [3]

The British, particularly after 1784, were acutely sensitive to possible invasion threats to India through the western and northwestern passes—the traditional invasion routes. The crea-

vii

PREFACE

tion of a strong, friendly Sikh state in the Punjab and the discovery that the much-feared Afghan ruler Zaman Shah was no more than a straw man tended to assuage British fears in the Northwest. The lower Indus Valley was a different matter. Sind, situated astride some of the major approaches to India, had been a much frequented invasion route. Although insulation by mountains and deserts and an abominable climate had usually preserved for it at least a semi-independent role, Sind's history had alternated between invasions from abroad and the rise and fall of indigenous dynasties. Traditionally Sind had been more of a passage way than a block to the invader. The Harappa civilization was overrun in the third millennium B.C. (probably by the Aryans). Alexander the Great passed through Sind, and it was the first province to receive the eighth-century Moslem onslaught. Sind fell to Mahmud of Ghazni in 1026. Akbar was born there and annexed it to the growing Moghul Empire in 1529. It was also in the sixteenth century that the Baluchis moved into Sind from the hills west of the Indus to become the governing class of the province. During the declining days of the Moghuls, a Baluchi tribe, the Kalhoras, established themselves as the rulers of Sind, first as tributaries of Delhi and then as independent chiefs. But they were soon conquered by Nadir Shah, and upon his death fell under the sway of the Durani kings of Afghanistan. In 1783, the Kalhoras were displaced by another Baluchi tribe, the Talpurs, with whom the British were destined to conduct their dealings. Mir Fatehali Khan, the chief architect of the Talpur victory, took over Lower Sind and ruled from its major city, Hyderabad, in conjunction with his three younger brothers.[4] Mir Sohrab Khan, a distant cousin of Mir Fatehali's founded a separated dynasty in Upper Sind with its capital at Khairpur; and the chief of another branch of the Talpurs, Mir Tharo Khan, established himself in Mirpur, in the extreme southeastern corner of Sind.

The expansion of British power in India at a time when the home authorities were strongly opposed to any further acquisi-

viii

PREFACE

tion of territory is one of the major paradoxes in the history of the nineteenth-century British Empire. British policy and activities in Sind between 1799 and 1843 veered from indifference to outright annexation, and the following pages will investigate the circumstances accompanying this radical shift in an attempt to delineate some of the motivations for imperial expansion in Sind, in India, and possibly in the rest of the empire.

I am most grateful to the many persons who have helped me in the preparation of this book and wish to thank particularly: Dr. Kenneth Ballhatchet of the School of Oriental and African Studies, University of London, the staff of the library of the University of California, Los Angeles, Mr. S. C. Sutton and the staff of the India Office Library in London, the personnel of the Public Record Office, the Keeper of the Records at the British Museum, the librarian of Nottingham University, Dr. P. M. Joshi and the staff of the Bombay Government Records Department, Dr. V. C. Joshi and the staff of the National Archives of India, Dr. M. Sadullah and the staff of the West Pakistan Historical Records Department in Lahore. Professor John S. Galbraith of the University of California, Los Angeles, under whose patient guidance I completed my graduate work, provided me with invaluable advice on the manuscript, as did Dr. Leo Rose and Dr. Margaret Fisher, my colleagues at the Center for South Asia Studies, University of California, Berkeley and Mr. R. I. Conhaim of the California Institute of Technology. Mr. H. T. Lambrick of Oriel College, Oxford, both personally and through his definitive study, *Sir Charles Napier and Sind*, made my task much easier. Finally, I am deeply indebted to the Fulbright Act authorities, to Professor Hallett Smith, chairman of the Humanities Division of the California Institute of Technology, and to the Ford Foundation without whose generous support this undertaking would not have been possible.

ROBERT A. HUTTENBACK
Pasadena, California

Contents

1. The French Threat (1799–1809)   1
2. The Controversy over Cutch (1814–1834)   13
3. The Establishment of British Preponderance (1834–1838)   30
4. The Afghan Crisis (1838–1841)   43
5. Ellenborough, Napier, and the Amirs of Sind (1841–1843)   68
6. The Annexation and Its Repercussions (1843–1850)   90
7. Conclusion   113
    Notes   123
    Bibliography   145
    Index   157

1. The French Threat
(1799–1809)

IN THE LAST YEARS of the eighteenth century the British Government watched the extension of French hegemony across Europe with growing alarm. Anxiety over the progress of events was not limited to the Continent, for Napoleon's successful invasion of Egypt kindled speculation as to the possibility of a French attack on India. The reconstituted East India Company, acutely sensitive to the vulnerability of the subcontinent, never realized the ephemeral nature of the supposed French and later Russian designs on its Eastern Empire.[1] Consequently, during the first half of the century virtually all British diplomatic, commercial, and military machinations in the countries to the west and northwest of India were directed toward the repulse of these anticipated threats.

As Napoleon had made no secret of his ambition to lead an army across Asia Minor to India, the authorities in both England and India became convinced of the imminence of the French menace. The young general's defeat outside Acre, the destruction of his fleet by Nelson, and the obvious logistical impracticality of marching a significant force through the arid and hostile lands of Southwest Asia did not diminish the determination of the Company's officers to bolster their military and diplomatic defenses in India.

Of prime importance to any defensive operation was the closing of Sind, which lay along the logical invasion route, not only to possible French intervention but also to the threatened schemes of the Marathas and Tipu Sultan of Mysore, who

1

THE FRENCH THREAT

was trying to ally himself with the amirs of Sind against the British. Zaman Shah, the King of Afghanistan, was likewise thought to be contemplating an invasion of India, possibly in coöperation with the French. Although a ruler of little consequence, he was excessively feared by the Company to whom the memory of Ahmad Shah was still green. It was anticipated that Zaman Shah might well march through Sind, which had nominally recognized Afghan suzerainty since 1757.

In direct response to these rumors, the Governor of Bombay,[2] Jonathan Duncan, at the behest of the Governor-General, the Marquis of Wellesley, in 1799 sent a merchant from Bushire to the court of Mir Fatehali Khan to try to set the stage for the restoration of amicable relations between Sind and British India.[3] The agent succeeded in his attempt because the amirs, frightened by the threat of the Kalhora pretender, Mian Abdul Nabi, to reconquer Sind, hoped that the British would offer them military aid both against him and their Afghan overlord in return for certain commercial concessions.

As a result of this mission Nathan Crow was sent to be the Company's agent in Sind. The Governor-General wrote to Duncan that a factory was to be established, "not so much with a view to commercial as to political advantages."[4] Its major function would be to supply information on the activities of Zaman Shah. Should the amirs permit the opening of the proposed Company establishment, Wellesley felt that the British for their part would be willing to make some minor concessions (unspecified in the letter) but not to the extent of rendering military aid to the amirs against their enemies.[5]

Crow landed at Karachi on March 2, 1800, and proceeded immediately to Hyderabad, where he was greeted in a friendly manner by Fatehali. The four amirs, despite their desire for British military support, at first suspected the Company of interest in conquest rather than commerce, but Crow assured them that he desired only "the removal of discord" and the increased trade and wealth the factory would bring to Sind.[6]

2

THE FRENCH THREAT

The amirs allowed themselves to become convinced; in time they granted the Company special rights at Karachi and Tatta,[7] as they hoped to increase the import of woolens from Rs. 50,000 to two lakhs.[8] When Crow left Hyderabad the amirs showered him with gifts; he confidently assured Bombay that Fatehali's fear of the Company had been assuaged and that while Crow had sought to conceal the prospect of making the Government of Sind "a political engine," he had seriously considered this possibility.[9] He then listed the advantages which he felt would be inherent in any British establishment in Sind: It would divert and worry Zaman Shah and make him more tractable; it would make Sindian help likely if attack on Afghanistan became necessary; it would make it possible for the British to foment a revolution against Kabul, if this proved necessary or desirable; it would preclude the entry of the French, Afghans, or Marathas; it would assure Sindian aid against the Marathas, who were after all infidels; it would be an excellent center from which to spy on Afghanistan, although this was currently impossible because of the close scrutiny under which the British party was being held. Only at the conclusion of his letter did Crow remark upon the commercial possibilities of the area.[10]

Crow had been excessively sanguine. The three junior amirs soon placed pressure on Fatehali, the chief of the Hyderabad Talpurs, for the speedy expulsion of the British, and he wrote to the Company's agent that he was beset on all sides.[11] Within a few days he issued an edict which closed the factory at Karachi and restricted the Company to Tatta and to Shahbunder, if they should wish to open a factory there. No more British ships were to be allowed at Karachi, and in future, although the Company would probably be allowed a Hindu agent there,[12] all imports would have to come through Kukrala.[13]

For a time it seemed as if Fatehali might reverse himself, as he personally favored the British connection, though his brother Ghulamali, the other two *Char Yar*, and various relatives were

3

opposed. But a threat from Fatehali's dreaded Afghan suzerain that he would invade Sind if the British were not expelled settled the issue,[14] and on October 28, 1800, Fatehali ordered Crow to remove himself and all the Company's establishments from Sind immediately. The agent had no choice but to comply, and, as insufficient time was allowed for the closing down of the factories and the settling of accounts, the East India Company lost Rs. 110,000 on the venture.

In a later period such an insult would have precipitated immediate retaliation. But with the inception of the Consulate and the renewal of the campaign against Austria, Napoleon became so tied up with affairs in Europe that even alarmist British statesmen were soon convinced that the French threat to India had at least temporarily waned. Thus the affairs of Sind no longer attracted disproportionate attention, especially as the British were preoccupied with their problems in Mysore and the Carnatic. The Company limited itself to demanding reparations from the amirs and showed no anxiety to repair the relations so abruptly severed. A suggestion by Jonathan Duncan to Wellesley that all Indian ports be closed to Sindian vessels and that all Sindian ports and merchandise currently in Indian ports be seized as compensation for Crow's expulsion and the resultant financial loss[15] was not implemented.

Fatehali Khan died in 1802 and was replaced as the principal amir of Hyderabad by his brother Ghulamali Khan. This formerly stout opponent of the Company's establishment in Sind soon attempted to reopen negotiations with the British, hoping that by a close relationship with them he might forestall an Afghan invasion of Sind, which he feared greatly.[16] He therefore sent an envoy to Bombay, but the local authorities would not receive him because of the unsettled British claims on Sind.

The Company was evidently not interested in pursuing an active policy to recoup its losses. Sir George Barlow, the Governor-General, in 1806 expressed the prevailing opinion when he wrote that the British Government thought it would be

4

"neither just nor expedient to have recourse to hostile measures for the purpose of avenging the insult offered to the British Government by the expulsion of Mr. Crow." But the Company also felt that relations should not be resumed until the claim was settled.[17]

When Lord Minto assumed the governor-generalship in 1807, he took a similar view. Previously as chairman of the Board of Control he had dedicated himself to the improvement of the Company's financial situation, and consequently he had opposed the extension of the British dominions in India. As Governor-General his views remained unaltered, and he was able to check at least temporarily the forward policy inaugurated by Wellesley. But the disintegration of the short-lived Peace of Amiens, 1803, had revived British apprehension as to possible French designs both on India and the area to the west of the Khyber Pass. The prospect of the French arousing anti-British feeling in the Northwest caused Minto to favor the use of Sind as an outpost for detecting possible French maneuvers. He wrote: "I do not allude at present to any expedition of any actual invasion of the British territories in India by a French army; but many considerations denote conclusively the extension of the enemy's views to this country." [18]

The conclusion of the Treaty of Tilsit in 1807 compounded already existing fears and raised the spectre of a combined Franco-Russian move on India through Persia, that country having turned to the French in 1805 after the British had failed to adhere to the treaty drawn up by General Malcolm in 1799. The home authorities became thoroughly alarmed and ordered the Governor-General to take measures to prevent a hostile army from crossing the Indus and to cultivate "to the utmost of your power the favourable opinion and cooperation not only of all states and countries to the Eastward of the Indus but also of the Afghan Government and even of the Tartar tribes to the Eastward of the Caspian." [19]

News soon reached Bombay that envoys from Sind had

THE FRENCH THREAT

arrived in Persia and had drawn up a treaty with the Shah under the terms of which the Persians were to aid the Sindians against the Afghans in return for the amirs' coöperation with the designs of the Persian king upon Kandahar. It was stated that the negotiations originated with the Sind agents.[20] Native intelligence agents forwarded similar rumors reporting the imminence of a French foothold in Sind, which, once established, would form links with Jodhpur and through it with Jaipur, Scindia, and other native states.[21]

Minto's reaction to this intelligence was immediate. He wrote to Bombay that "dispatches from N. H. Smith at Bushire telling us of the visit of the Sind Vakeels to Persia and the French overtures to Sind have convinced the Government of the expediency of reopening relations with Sind." [22] Minto declared that the demand for reparations must be overlooked in the light of greater considerations and that Bombay should immediately send an emissary to Sind. The envoy should demand an indemnity from the amirs but only to embarrass them and to give the British a psychological advantage. He should of course be accompanied by an escort which would give "might and consequence to a diplomatic mission." If the amirs refused the demand for the establishment of a factory, an agent at least should be insisted upon. If both requests were granted, the offices of resident and Company district officer in charge of the factory should be kept rigidly separated so that the agent could devote his full time to political matters. The main duty of the agent must be to determine the extent of the Franco-Sind relationship and to counteract it by all means possible. He should attempt to determine the extent of the Franco-Persian influence in the countries north of Sind and do his utmost to reëstablish British influence in the Sind court. The Governor-General also suggested that the agent investigate the feasibility of an army's marching from India to Persia. He concluded by emphasizing that thus far his recommendations were to be considered as only tentative and that they had been forwarded merely for the presidency's consideration.[23]

By coincidence both Ghulamali and Duncan had determined independently to try to reëstablish amicable relations between the Company and Sind. Through the efforts of two employees of the Bombay Government, an agent sent to Bombay by Ghulamali was persuaded to request an emissary from Bombay to accompany him to Hyderabad. Duncan promptly appointed Captain David Seton, the British resident at Muscat, to do so.

Seton left Bombay in April, 1808, accompanied by his chief aide Lieutenant Grindley, an assistant surgeon, and an officer in charge of sixty rank of native infantry.[24] He was instructed to gain the confidence of the amirs in order to promote the Company's aims of setting up a factory and of acquiring permission for the reception of a political envoy in Sind. Seton was to use the Company's claim for an indemnity of Rs. 70,000 as a means of gaining concessions from the amirs, and he was to extend his enquiries northward, but with discretion, so as not to arouse the suspicions of Ghulamali.[25]

Seton arrived at Mandavi in Cutch on May 18 and remained there for about six weeks. This greatly distressed Duncan, who wanted him to arrive in Hyderabad before the Persian emissary. But Fateh Ali Khan, the Persian envoy, reached Hyderabad on June 4 and was received with the highest honors. Fateh Ali was reported to have offered Franco-Persian help to Sind in shaking off the shackles of Afghan overlordship in return for the use of Sindian ports and facilities to supply French ships. He pointed out that the British by their growing dominance in India had become a danger to world peace and that it was Ghulamali's duty to aid in the elimination of this hazard.[26] In addition he brought with him a proclamation from the King of Persia appointing Ghulamali *baylarbey*[27] of Kabul and Kandahar as a reward for his coöperation.[28] The amirs also received communications to the same effect from Joseph Rousseau, the French resident in Baghdad.[29]

7

The dilatory Seton finally arrived in Hyderabad on June 15, 1808, and a week later had a conference with Ghulamali who, realizing the strength of his position, declared that had the English not sent Seton "to cultivate his friendship, he would in despair of gaining their good will have closed with the offer of the French and the Persians." [30] The Amir proposed a treaty containing mutual assistance clauses and a provision permitting the British to reopen factories at Tatta and Hyderabad. Other articles provided that neither government should protect the enemies of the other, that the British should provide Ghulamali with artillery for the capture of Umarkot, eighty miles east of Hyderabad, which he said belonged by right to Sind, and that British and Sind divide between them the coastal province of Cutch, which lay just to the east of Sind.[31]

Seton agreed to these terms, with the exception of those referring to Umarkot and Cutch. He also dropped all Company claims for reparations against Sind. Seton felt that his actions were in keeping with his mission to reëstablish relations with Sind and to undermine Russian, French, and Persian influence at all costs.[32]

In consonance with the rest of his instructions Seton tried to reopen communications with the states to the north of Sind. When an emissary from Shah Shuja, successor to Zaman Shah as ruler of Afghanistan, arrived in Hyderabad to collect past tribute from the amirs, Seton entrusted the envoy with a letter to the King warning him of the dangers of allying himself with the French.[33] But before the messenger could leave Hyderabad, Ghulamali learned of Seton's missive and forced the Company's agent to withdraw it. Undismayed, Seton promptly sent it again through Kuwal Muzaffer Khan, the Governor of Multan, who was returning from a pilgrimage to Mecca, and to make sure that at least one letter got through to Shah Shuja, he sent two more copies from Mandavi to Cutch. The amirs now became increasingly disenchanted with the British. Not only had Seton made overtures to Shah Shuja, whose yoke on Sind the

THE FRENCH THREAT

amirs were trying to break, but he had interfered in palace politics. To make matters worse Mian Abdul Nabi again appeared on the scene. He was in Jodhpur claiming strong support in Sind and seeking British aid in regaining his throne.[34]

Meanwhile the authorities in India and England expressed strong disapproval of Seton's actions.[35] Both Minto and Duncan were shocked that Seton had agreed to the mutual defense clauses in the new agreement.[36] Minto was particularly incensed by the cumbersome attempts to communicate with the ruler of Afghanistan.[37] Much of this criticism was unfair. As Seton himself said, he had been sent to Sind to counteract Franco-Persian intrigue, and he had used the only means at hand.[38] He had not been informed that Minto had decided to send secret missions to Lahore, Kabul, and Persia[39] to establish an alliance system with these border states, and that hence Seton's clumsy machinations were out of place.[40]

Now the British Government was faced with the unenviable task of reversing the terms of the treaty without unduly affronting the amirs. The difficulties were compounded by the delay engendered by the loss, *en route*, of the first copy of the treaty Seton had sent to Bombay. Minto decided that Seton should not disavow his own agreement. He planned to send Nicholas Hankey Smith, the British agent at Bushire, to Sind as the representative of the Central Government, for the Governor-General felt that this would be in accord with the new policy of sending agents deputed directly to Fort William to the north and west of Sind. As he pointed out, it would be foolish to send an envoy to Kabul and at the same time to adhere to a treaty which pledged support to the Sindians in throwing off the Afghan overlordship. The treaty could be rescinded by telling the amirs that Seton was merely the representative of the Bombay presidency, and that the treaty had not been ratified by the Governor-General, who was now sending his own emissary.[41] Minto wrote to Ghulamali that he intended to

9

afford the Amir the strongest testimony of the friendly disposition of the British Government

by removing the veil of intermediate authority and opening a direct communication between the Supreme Government and the State of Scind. . . . From this measure you will duly appreciate the extent of my inclination to remove all former grounds of misunderstanding and permanently to establish the foundations of harmony and friendship between the two states.[42]

Duncan soon wrote to Ghulamali to restate the Governor-General's case. He again went over the reasons for sending Smith to Hyderabad. "I feel persuaded," he concluded,

that, in view of the illustrious, and supreme authority from which this deputation proceeds, Your Excellency will not fail duly to appreciate its superior advantages to both Governments and the greater Credit, in particular, thereby reflected on your own, in having now to treat immediately with the representative of the fountain and the source of all British authority in the East.[43]

On November, 28, Neil B. Edmonstone, then secretary to the Central Government, sent Smith his instructions. He was to place British relations with Sind on the footing originally intended, which would necessitate his coming to an agreement with the amirs to supersede Seton's. The British could obviously enter into no agreement with Sind which would include military aid against Afghanistan. If the amirs were refractory, Smith should revive the indemnity claims and hint at possible British aid to the Afghans against Sind and support of the Kalhora pretender. His mission was intended "to embrace a general superintendence of the British interest in that country as are proximately or remotely connected with the meditated projects of our European enemies against the British possessions in India." [44] Smith was to have jurisdiction not only in Sind but

THE FRENCH THREAT

in the neighboring countries as well, and he was to conduct geographic investigations wherever feasible. He was to take with him an officer to command an escort of forty to fifty sepoys who should have some knowledge of surveying, and he and the doctor should be capable of conducting "local researches." Young Henry Pottinger, at that time an ensign in the service of the Company, was included in the party.[45]

Smith arrived at Karachi in June and—after many delays and the exchange of numerous acrimonious letters—proceeded to Hyderabad. The amirs were not very cordial and of course objected to the abrogation of Seton's treaty. Smith thought them "capricious and ignorant": they could not see the benefits to themselves of an East India Company factory and demanded "some advantage of equal value and importance."[46] He later wrote to Calcutta that he had explained to the amirs that "the right possessed by a state to disavow the acts of a public agent exceeding or acting contrary to his instructions is indisputable" and that he was "happy to say that the mode of explanation adopted had the desired effect, as the complaints of the Sind Government upon the subject of the Quolnama [treaty] have now entirely ceased."[47] The amirs stated that the establishment of a factory depended upon the British coöperation in their designs upon Cutch. If the British would not help, they should at least not interfere; in return for this the amirs would sign an offensive-defensive treaty against the French but would not allow the factory.[48] Smith implied that the British mission to Kabul indicated an impending *rapprochement* with Afghanistan, but this was an empty gesture because of Mahomed Shah's recent defeat of Shah Shuja. Smith intimated to the amirs that their designs on Cutch were impossible and tried vainly to substitute in the minds of the rulers the idea of a British political residency for that of a commercial one.[49]

Opposition to Smith's mission was directed at the amirs from all sides. The emissaries of the Rajah of Jodhpur and Bahawal Khan urged Ghulamali to dismiss the British envoys as they

11

were in Sind only to obtain geographical information as a prelude to domination. They pointed out that Sind was the only country bordering India that had not yet fallen under British sway. These arguments impressed the amirs, and they prepared to dismiss Smith who anticipated this insult by asking for permission to depart.[50]

It was Ghulamali's plan to minimize British influence in Sind but at the same time not to force the Company into coercive measures by complete refusal of its terms; therefore he still insisted that the establishment of a factory in Sind was dependent upon British aid against Cutch and announced his intention of writing to the Governor-General on the matter. He was willing, however, to allow an annual exchange of missions, and to permit a native of India to remain in Hyderabad on behalf of the British. He also promised to reject any overtures from the French and in fact dismissed the envoy of the Maratha leader, Juswunt Rao Holkar of Indore, who wished Sind to join him in alliance with the French.[51] Smith agreed to these terms mainly because he could obtain no better and because he felt that the treaty would at least achieve the primary purpose of his mission, that of excluding the French from Sind without obligating the British to render military aid to Ghulamali against Afghanistan.[52]

The treaty was signed in August, 1809,[53] and its ratification assuaged British fears in regard to a possible French foothold on the subcontinent. The realization that Napoleon, enmeshed in dynastic intrigues and unable to extricate himself from the Iberian Peninsula, posed no further threat to India soon returned the affairs of Sind to their original obscurity. The Secret Committee considered the peaceful situation reason "of the most forcible nature for proceeding without unnecessary delay, to reduce our military expenses within the narrowest bounds that may be consistent with the publick security and interests." [54]

2. The Controversy over Cutch
(1814–1834)

THE *Char Yar* GREATLY EXTENDED Hyderabad's dominions. Karachi was obtained from Kelat; Umarkot, formerly a part of Sind, from Jodhpur; part of the southeastern desert from the Rajput Sodhas (in conjunction with the Upper Sind amirs); and Shikarpur from Afghanistan. The amirs' ambitions also extended to Cutch. But here their interests clashed with those of the British Government, which was slowly increasing its own influence in Cutch, largely in order to suppress the pirates and banditti based there who constantly harried British trade and border posts.[1]

The Sindian claims on Cutch did not abate despite the repeated rejection of these claims by the British. Sir Evan Napean, Governor of Bombay in 1814, wrote that the Sind Government was inimical to the English and might even be encouraging the pirates. The amirs, he felt, must be forced to keep their hands off Cutch.[2] Lord Moira answered that Cutch should, if possible, be encouraged to control the pirates itself. But the Governor-General did not

consider it under the circumstances of the times, to be an object of such paramount importance as to justify the measures of war and expenses to which an attack on Cutch by the Rulers of Scind in opposition to our declared resolution would necessarily lead. In the present state of our relations with Cutch also, we cannot but feel the peculiar awkwardness and inconsistency of engaging in its defence, in hostilities with another state.[3]

The official attitude, however, was soon to change. In 1814 Bombay sent Colonel Holmes with a force to check the predators,[4] and treaties signed in 1816 and 1819 virtually made Cutch a British dependency. The Company's protection of Cutch set them against the Khosa tribe, which made frequent raids on Cutch and then returned to the safety of Parkur, in the dominions of the amirs of Hyderabad. The British often demanded that the amirs restrain their refractory subjects but usually to little effect, and early in 1820 the Company found it necessary to send a force under Lieutenant Colonel Barclay to suppress the Khosas, all else having failed. It so happened that the amirs had also sent some troops to achieve the same purpose; and just as the Sindian forces made contact with the Khosas, Barclay arrived upon the scene and, thinking that both groups were tribesmen, attacked, killing several Sindians as well as Khosas.

The amirs promptly retaliated by sending a force to raid Luna in Cutch and a series of hostile exchanges ensued. The amirs threatened a full-scale invasion of Cutch if the British did not apologize, and they suggested that a British envoy armed with appropriate letters be sent to Sind.[5] The Bombay Government replied that the attack on the Sindians had been an unfortunate accident "owing to [the British] being confronted by a large body of Khosas whom [the Sindians] had imprudently admitted to their camp." The Bombay Government was sorry but they could not give the amirs satisfaction until they had removed their forces from Cutch.[6]

Francis Warden, the secretary of the Bombay Government, wrote to Charles Metcalfe, then secretary in the secret and political departments at Fort William, to explain the situation:

By an unfortunate mistake, as much to be attributed to the misconduct of the Scindian Commander, in giving refuge to the Khosas within his camp, as to any other cause, a body of Scindians was attacked on a dark night by one of our detachments and many of the troops comprising it cut to pieces.[7]

The British had been inclined to make some sort of restitution, he continued, but the amirs had attacked Luna without waiting. Now the Bombay Government would be willing to let matters rest were it not for the fact they felt such a course would most surely lead to war either in the present or in the future. Hence a small fine should be levied on the amirs, after the payment of which the British might pay an indemnity for the attack on the Sindians. If the amirs did not agree to these terms, Warden suggested that the British commence hostilities against them.[8]

Mountstuart Elphinstone, the Governor of Bombay, expanded on Warden's views and in general acted in a most uncharacteristic manner. The British must act against the Sindian invasion, he wrote. Though Barclay's assault was a mistake and his explanation had been accepted by the amirs, they had nonetheless attacked. They had pillaged and burned a village and carried off some of the inhabitants as prisoners and had followed this with menacing letters and by a display of an intent to invade Cutch with their entire force. Now the amirs must pay one to two lakhs to the rao[9] as compensation. Once the amirs did this, the British might pay them an indemnity as recompense for Barclay's attack. But in both cases the British would set the amount, the latter "being a voluntary remuneration for an accident and the other exacted satisfaction for an intentional act." [10] If the amirs refused, the Governor intended to wage war on Sind until they agreed. He thought that an army of 10,000 infantry and 2,000 cavalry with a field train and horse artillery, as well as adequate supplies and stores would be sufficient to carry out the operation successfully. In addition, a cruiser and steam boats should be stationed on the Run (an inland arm of the sea) to protect Cutch and to harass Sindian weak points.[11] The Bombay Government felt that the expenses of the proposed war would be inconsiderable, especially in view of the probable effect "which it is hoped . . . will be so important." [12]

CONTROVERSY OVER CUTCH

The reaction of the Governor-General to these bellicose proposals was immediate. The political secretary to the Government wrote:

Few things in his Lordship's judgment can be conceived to be more impolitic than War with Sind. Not to dwell on the expense and unprofitableness of such an undertaking, or the chances of failure inseparable from all human enterprises, it is evident that the most prosperous result of War with Sind would be an evil as tending to involve us in disputes, jealousies, enmities, intrigues, negotiations, wars and incalculable embarrassments in the Countries beyond the Indus.[13]

The British, he continued, should consolidate their power within its present sphere, although the future might force expansion into other lands in self-defense. The Governor-General thought the terms proposed by Bombay fair, but he would not agree to their enforcement. War, if it came, must be provoked by Sind, and although it was the duty of the British Government to protect its subjects from plunderers and the depredations of the Sind Government, "the Governor-General in Council anxiously hopes that our obligation to our subjects and allies may be fulfilled without involving us in a most impolitic War." [14]

Bombay, still convinced that hostilities were imminent, continued to prepare for war; a stinging rebuke from the Governor-General resulted. He wrote:

There seems to be a conception which the Governor General in Council thinks inaccurate that we are the only injured party in the business. No person a distance [sic] will admit the discrimination assumed between the outrage committed on our part and that which followed on the part of the Sindians.[15]

Moira urged an investigation of Barclay's actions to show the amirs that the British were well-intentioned; and he pointed

16

CONTROVERSY OVER CUTCH

out that a war with Sind would not only be expensive but useless, because there was not a single feature in the land whose capture would bring the amirs to their knees. The Governor-General also felt obliged to remark on the reasoning resorted to by Bombay in claiming that preparations for war once undertaken could not be relaxed:

Tho' they have been begun without authority from this Government—the admission of such an excuse would completely destroy the checks which the Legislature has placed the Supreme Government of India for preventing the Presidencies of Fort St. George and Bombay from engaging in hostilities on their view of circumstances.[16]

The Governor-General's castigation had the desired effect, and it was a much chastened Warden who wrote to James Williams, the acting resident in Cutch, that he was sure war could be avoided and the existing difficulties with Sind settled amicably.[17] Accordingly, a Sindian delegation was sent to Bombay, and a treaty was signed on November 9, 1820, providing for eternal friendship between the contracting parties, the exclusion of Americans and Europeans from Sind, the mutual exchange of *vakils* (ambassadors), and the control of the Khosas by the amirs.[18]

Elphinstone still insisted that only the preparations for war and a display of strength by the British had prevented hostilities,[19] but he sent Captain Saddler on a mission to Sind "to be conducted on the lowest scale consistent with respectability . . . as a proof that the advances of the Ameers had not been rejected."[20] Saddler was instructed to conduct himself in a most friendly manner and to be cautious about mentioning the matter of the freebooters. Even the procuring of geographical or statistical information should be avoided, if there was any chance of exciting the suspicions of the amirs.[21]

Despite some recurrence of the old problems in 1825, the

17

Anglo-Sind troubles in Cutch were largely a closed chapter after the conclusion of the treaty. Moira, over the opposition of Elphinstone, had shown that at least in this instance he agreed with the Board of Control and the Secret Committee that "no further acquisition of territory can be desirable." [22]

Intercourse with Sind assumed a new importance when fear of foreign invasion in the late 1820's again emphasized the strategic importance of the area. Lord Ellenborough, who in 1829 had become chairman of the Board of Control in the Wellington Government, dreaded a combined Russo-Persian move on India, as the Persians, disappointed by the British failure to adhere to the treaty of 1814, had concluded a treaty with the Russians. He wrote: "The Directors are much afraid of the Russians, so am I. . . . I feel confident we shall have to fight the Russians on the Indus."[23] His apprehensions coincided with the publication of Colonel De Lacey Evans's book, *On the Designs of Russia*,[24] which appeared in 1829. Evans explained in detail how the Russians could effect a successful invasion of India through Afghanistan; and although most of his conclusions were based on faulty assumptions, the work greatly impressed both Ellenborough and Wellington. As a result, the former wrote in his diary that should the Russians occupy Khiva the British would have to capture Lahore and if need be Kabul, and to achieve this purpose the Indian army should be increased to 70,000 men and complete control of the Indus assumed.[25]

If Evans's book aroused renewed interest in Sind through the negative factor of fear, the report, *A Narrative of a Visit to the Court of Sinde*, written by Dr. James Burnes as a result of his trip to Sind in 1827 to minister to the chief amir, Murad Ali Khan, was to have an even greater influence on the determination of future British policy. In it, for the first time, the potentialities of the Indus and of Sind itself were assessed, though somewhat optimistically and inaccurately. Burnes strongly advocated British control of the region:

CONTROVERSY OVER CUTCH

The river Indus might once more become the channel of communication and wealth between the interior of Asia and the peninsula of India; while Sinde herself . . . would rise renewed to claim a due importance in the scale of nations, and to profit by her benefits which nature has bestowed on her. . . . A single glance at the Indus will show the easy passage to the very heart of their [the amirs'] dominions, which the river offers to a maritime power.[26]

The Indus was actually a poor avenue of communication. It was constantly silting up, and its course, impeded by sand bars and shallows, changed considerably from year to year. This fact was not realized for some time, however, and for the moment the thought of opening the Indus captured the imagination of the officials of Albemarle and Leadenhall [27] streets. Ellenborough was particularly affected. He wrote: "No British flag has ever floated upon the waters of this river! Please God it shall, and in triumph, to the source of all its tributary streams." [28]

Ellenborough was as much concerned about the peaceful intrusion of Russian merchants into Central Asia as he was about the threat of actual military invasion. He thought that the opening of the Indus would encourage British traders to replace their Russian counterparts,[29] and he intended to obtain full information on Russian activities in the countries between the Caspian and the Indus.[30]

If official interest in England had now become directed toward the Indus Valley, so had that in India itself. With the appointment of Lord William Bentinck as Governor-General in 1828 the reins of government were in the hands of a Benthamite utilitarian who was not blind to the commercial possibilities of the Indus. No doubt he too had read the books by Burnes and Evans. The Company as usual advised the new Governor-General to be vigilant about costs and to avoid territorial expansion. William Astall, one of the "chairs," wrote to Bentinck:

19

The expenses of [the Indian Establishment] are now under consideration and I trust that they may be greatly reduced without injury to the public interests—and I would fain hope and believe that under your Lordship's administration, if Peace and Tranquility be preserved in India, the embarrassments in which the Company's affairs are now involved will be removed and that we shall be able to render a good account of our government of India both as respects our Financial and Political administration.[31]

The "chairs" were, however, "desirous of being much better informed than we are now as to the actual state of Scind . . . particularly as to the navigation of the Main Stream of the Indus." [32]

Ellenborough decided that, as a preliminary step to the opening of the Indus, the river would have to be at least rudimentarily surveyed. Although previous attempts to do so had been frustrated by the amirs, who feared that British knowledge of the river would invite occupation, Ellenborough found a way to disguise his purpose. Ranjit Singh had sent a present to William IV at the time of his coronation; Ellenborough now proposed to reciprocate by sending a gift of one dray horse and four dray mares to the ruler of the Punjab on behalf of the British monarch. The horses would of course be accompanied by an emissary who would "assume no ostensible character but that of an Agent deputed solely for arranging the Safe Passage of the Horses and of presenting them to Ranjeet Singh." [33] The real purpose would be to survey the Indus and its tributary streams from its mouth to Lahore and to obtain the support of Ranjit Singh for the British commercial schemes on the Indus. The Company hoped that the produce of both England and India could be sent up the Indus to points of entrepôt from where it could be transshipped to the markets of Afghanistan and Persia. It was thought that in this way the British would not only undersell the Russians but could obtain for themselves a large portion of the trade of Central Asia.[34]

CONTROVERSY OVER CUTCH

The Governor-General decided to send Lieutenant Alexander Burnes, brother of the doctor, to head the expedition. He had been engaged in a survey of the Northwest frontier at the time the idea was conceived and hence was considered well qualified. Ensign Leckie was to accompany him, and the destination of the presents was to be kept secret until the boats bearing them had left Mandavi. Then letters were to be sent to the amirs, "but so as to arrive too late to prevent the receipt of any answer having for its object the prevention of the mission, until the boats shall have advanced too far to admit of being stopped." [35] To insure the passage of the presents by the river a large carriage was added to the consignment.[36] The amirs were to be told that the presents had to go by water because of their size. Progress was to be slow to allow for a full survey of the river. Only Charles Metcalfe, now a member of the Governor-General's Council, sounded a note to dampen the general enthusiasm. He wrote:

The scheme for surveying the Indus under the pretence of sending a present to Rajah Ranjeet Singh seems to be highly objectionable. It is a trick, in my opinion unworthy of our government, which cannot fail when detected, as most probably it will be, to excite the jealousy and indignation of the powers on whom we play it. It is just such a trick, as we are often falsely suspected and accused of by the Native Powers of India, and this confirmation of their suspicions, generally unjust, will do us more injury by furnishing the ground of merited reproach than any advantage to be gained by the measure can compensate. . . .

Twenty years ago the writer of this minute was employed to negotiate an alliance against a French invasion, with a native state beyond our Northwestern Frontier. A French invasion was our Bugbear then as a Russian one is now.[37]

But Metcalfe's was a voice in the wilderness and preparations for sending the presents to Ranjit Singh continued.

Burnes sailed from Bombay in 1830 and made two attempts to land in Sind during January and February, 1831, but the amirs would not let the mission proceed. They used several excuses such as the presence of bandits and the lack of water in the Indus, which would necessitate the expedition going overland.[38] The amirs remained adamantly in opposition for over a month, but on March 20, Henry Pottinger, the British agent in Cutch, reported to Bombay that the amirs, prompted by British threats to reopen the matter of the Khosa depredations, and a military demonstration on their border by Ranjit Singh's general, Ventura, had agreed to let the mission pass.[39] Burnes now started on his journey up the Indus and was favorably received by the amirs of Hyderabad and Khairpur as well as by Ranjit Singh himself. During Burnes's journey a *syed*[40] supposedly said: "Alas! Sinde is now gone since the English have seen the river, which is the road to its conquest."[41] Burnes in the narrative of his journey wrote: "There is an uninterrupted navigation from the sea to Lahore. . . . The Indus when joined by the Punjab Rivers never shallows in the dry season to less than fifteen feet."[42] Burnes's report was enthusiastically received, for little was known of his predilection for gross exaggeration. Pottinger, who knew the area well and was aware of the inaccuracies and inadequacies of Burnes's comments, limited himself to stating: "*I do* differ from many of the facts and opinions stated by Lieutenant Burnes."[43] Bentinck wrote to Bombay: "The result (of Burnes's mission) has satisfied me that the importance of the River Indus in a political point of view not less than as a route of commerce has not been overrated."[44] He further informed Lord Clare, the Governor of Bombay, that Pottinger had been deputed to start negotiations with the amirs on the matter of opening the Indus.[45]

Pottinger received his instructions from the Governor-General in October, 1831. He was to negotiate only with Murad Ali of Hyderabad and Rustam Khan of Khairpur, and he should use the implied threat of Ranjit Singh on their northern border and the continued depredations of the Khosas as a means of achieving his ends if the amirs were recalcitrant. He might also cite Vattel's law under which straits could not be closed by the controlling power; although this would entail the necessity of defining the Indus as a strait between the sea and the British possessions in the Northwest, a rather strained usage at best. Henry Prinsep, one of the Governor-General's secretaries, pointed out to Pottinger:

The Secret Committee of the Honorable Court of Directors have expressed great anxiety to obtain the free navigation of the Indus with a view to the advantages that might result from substituting our own influence for that derived by Russia, through her commercial intercourse with Bokhara in the countries lying between Hindustan and the Caspian Sea, as well as because of the great facilities afforded by the River for the disposal of produce and manufactures of the British dominions both in Europe and in India.[46]

The mission arrived in Sind in early January, 1832, and was courteously welcomed by Murad Ali. Negotiations centered on the right of British and Indian merchants to use the Indus. Pottinger made telling use of the Khosa issue and the threat of Ranjit Singh who, he pointed out, might descend on Sind unless the amirs had come to some previous agreement with the British.[47] On February 3, Pottinger submitted to Murad Ali his draft of the proposed treaty, which essentially provided for the opening of the Indus to the merchants and traders of India.[48] But before the conclusion of the treaty with Hyderabad Pottinger proceeded to Khairpur to draw up a treaty with Mir Rustam Khan, although Murad Ali claimed that Khairpur was subordinate to Hyderabad and hence covered by any treaty signed by himself. Pottinger's first draft of the proposed treaty with Khairpur provided for eternal friendship between the British Government and Khairpur; free navigation of the portion of the Indus within the boundaries of the state of Khairpur was to be ceded to the British Government for the use of its merchants and traders; a system of equitable duties was to be set up, and the friendly relations between the two states was to be cemented by the sending of ambassadors from time to time.[49]

The intention of the envoy had been to keep the negotiations between the British and Khairpur on a separate footing from those with Hyderabad despite the latter's claim of superior status. This turned out to be impossible because of the insistence of Rustam's brother, Mir Mubarak Khan, and for that matter of Rustam himself that Khairpur and Hyderabad were closely connected. Pottinger now prepared another version of the treaty which added to the provisions of the first draft, "that the two Governments refrain from casting the eye of covetousness on the possessions of each other." [50] But Pottinger still had not taken into account the relationship between Khairpur and Hyderabad, and when the Upper Sind amirs, particularly Mubarak, insisted that no treaty was necessary and that any treaty with Hyderabad would bind Khairpur, Pottinger produced a third draft which added a clause:

The British Government having requested the free navigation of the river, as well as the roads of the Country for its traders and merchants, the Government of Khyrpoor (namely Meer Roostum Khan) grants the same as his boundaries extend on whatever terms may be settled with the Government of Hyderabad.[51]

The treaty, signed on April 4, 1832, provided for continuing friendly relations between Khairpur and the British. The merchants of Hindustan were granted the use of the river and roads of Khairpur on whatever terms might be settled with "the Government of Hyderabad, namely Meer Murad Ali Khan Talpoor" [52] and the Government of Khairpur promised to provide the British with a statement of just and reasonable tolls to be levied and not to hinder the traders in any way.[53] Pottinger

CONTROVERSY OVER CUTCH

"casually adverted to the advantage that might spring to Khyrpoor as far as the Sikhs were concerned by having a Resident Agent on the part of the British Government" in Khairpur.[54] But Rustam replied that he was not afraid of the Sikhs and would prefer an offensive-defensive alliance, which it was clearly against current British policy to sign.[55]

Pottinger returned to Hyderabad on April 16 to conclude the treaty negotiations. He promptly rejected a treaty draft sent him by Murad Ali which provided, among other things, that the British should inform Kabul and the Sikh Government that Sind was to be respected in future as if it were British territory.[56] But he managed to convince Murad Ali that the British were not conniving with Ranjit Singh against Sind, the suspicion of which had prompted the amirs' fears of British intercourse with Khairpur, and the treaty was signed on April 20, 1832.

Its provisions were, in the main, identical to those in the treaty with Khairpur:[57] Merchants from Hindustan were to be allowed to travel from one country to another along the Indus providing that no military stores were transported by the rivers or roads of Sind, that no armed vessel or boat should travel on the river, and that no Englishman be permitted to settle in Sind; all merchants visiting Sind would have to get a British passport, and the Hyderabad authorities would have to be informed of the granting of such a document; the Sind Government would fix an equitable and fair table of duties and would not delay merchants; those parts of former treaties not amended by the present one would still remain in effect, and the two countries would exchange emissaries whenever it was necessary or desirable.[58] On the same day a supplemental treaty of three articles was signed which provided for the levying of the duties discussed in Article 5 of the perpetual treaty and for the joint action of Sindian, British, and Jodhpur troops for the suppression of the Parkur and Thull freebooters.[59]

Toward the end of June Bentinck returned the ratified treaties with Khairpur and Hyderabad to Pottinger, who now, in addi-

25

tion to his duties as resident in Cutch, was to have charge of Sind affairs. The British had not achieved all their aims, however, notably the acceptance of British residents at Hyderabad and Khairpur. Clare thought that "without some British officer on the spot to settle disputes our Traders will be exposed to endless difficulties." [60]

Nonetheless the agreement of Ranjit Singh and Bahawal Khan opened the Indus to commerce. With the conclusion of the treaties an experimental cargo was sent up the river, and in 1833 a group of merchants sailed boats down the Indus from Ludhiana to Shikapur; but results were disappointing. The difficulties of navigating the river, the threat of predatory tribes along its banks in Upper Sind, and the general lack of commercial activity in the area precluded success.

The British authorities attributed the at least temporary failure of the experiment to their insufficient control of the Indus. In consequence of this, C. E. Trevelyan, a deputy secretary to the Government in Calcutta, drew up a paper on the Indus tariff at the Governor-General's request. He pointed out that transportation by water was much cheaper than by land and that the duty levied by the amirs should be on the value of the cargo rather than on weight. Cargo should be taxed only once on the trip, and the proceeds should be divided among Sind, Bahawalpur, Lahore, and British India; while the collection of the toll should be under the superintendence of a British political agency.[61] Bentinck, for his part, favored the negotiation of a new treaty with the amirs which would give the British greater influence in Sind. He wrote: "I could wish that it may be accomplished without the employment of direct force, but by the effect of other and milder influences." [62]

Again only Metcalfe opposed the plan. He said it would require a control of the river which the British neither had nor had a right to expect.[63] Pottinger now wrote a minute in which he expressed the opinion that the amirs were taxing trade out of existence and that Murad Ali was trying to make the recent

CONTROVERSY OVER CUTCH

treaty a dead letter by means of excessive duties. He thought a toll based on the size of each boat should be levied:

I intend [that] the British Government should assume a dictatorial tone on this occasion and it will by so doing, neither invade nor injure any existing right or property, it is bound, I conceive to place the whole matter, at once, on a foundation commensurate with the high interest at stake.[64]

The Governor-General agreed with the advisability of replacing the duty with a toll but cautioned Pottinger that in conducting negotiations he should give

the Ameers every assurance that the internal trade of their own country will not be interfered with. The moment goods are landed at Tatta, Hyderabad or anywhere else in their dominions they will become subject to the local duties levied by the Ameers in their own country.[65]

But the amirs were not to interfere with foreign trade, and Pottinger should attempt to gain permission for the establishment of a British agent at the mouths of the Indus.[66]

In October, 1833, Murad Ali died and was succeeded by his eldest son, Nur Mahomed, as the principal chief of Lower Sind. He firmly refused to allow the creation of a British residency in Sind. Pottinger was at a loss about what to do as his instructions forbade him to "demand anything or to use coercion."[67] He could only retaliate by refusing to draw up separate treaties with the various amirs recognizing their independent positions, because with the death of Murad Ali, the last of the *Char Yar*, the chief amir was only to be *primus inter pares*.

The amirs continued steadfastly to refuse their permission for the creation of the residency and evinced no enthusiasm about signing any new treaty. Pottinger wrote:

27

Unless we mean to abandon the great Design of opening the Indus to traffic, we must, in the event I am contemplating, change our Requests to Demands and support those demands, by increasing the Force in Kutch and blockading the ports of Sinde till everything we wish is fully acceded to.[68]

To Nur Mahomed he stated that the intended treaty constituted no interference with the internal trade of Sind:

It is clearly understood, that should goods at any time be landed from boats at Tattah, Hyderabad, Sehwan, Khyrpoor, or any other place within the territories of the governments of Hyderabad and Khyrpoor, they will instantly become subject to all duties levied by those Governments and in which, the British Government has no wish or intention to interfere.[69]

Still the amirs would not conclude a new agreement; and W. Macnaghten, the other secretary to the Governor-General, finally wrote Pottinger that if the amirs failed to sign any of the treaty drafts, action on the order suggested by Pottinger would result.[70] Even the pacifically inclined Bentinck informed the Secret Committee that, since the amirs had refused to sign a treaty to which, he claimed, they had already agreed (although there is no evidence of any such acquiescence), he had authorized the agent in Sind:

to intimate to [the amirs] distinctly that unless within a reasonable period (to be fixed by that officer) they fulfilled the engagements which had been solemnly contracted in the matter of the Treaty, we should be compelled to adopt measures of coercion, as might be necessary to insure their compliance.[71]

But financial considerations precluded any armed intervention in Sind, and the treaty signed between the East India Company and the amirs on July 2, 1834, did not fulfill British expectations. It provided for a uniform toll on all boats traveling on the Indus

CONTROVERSY OVER CUTCH

of which Tatta Rs. 240 would accrue to Hyderabad and Khairpur and the rest be divided between the Company, Lahore, and Bahawalpur. A native agent was to be stationed at the mouths of the Indus to assist in the collection of tolls and to arbitrate disputes; if necessary a British officer could from time to time come to Sind to settle any difficulties.[72] The British were thus at least temporarily frustrated in their design of stationing an agent at Hyderabad, but events were soon to present an opportunity for the revision of existing engagements.

3. The Establishment
of British Preponderance
(1834–1838)

BRITISH ACTIVITY in Sind after the treaty of 1834 was directed toward the attainment of three objectives: the conducting of a full survey of the Indus, the encouragement of increased commerce on the river, and the establishment of a residency in Sind. These goals were all achieved within the next four years with the indirect aid of Ranjit Singh.

In May, 1835, Pottinger had sent his assistant, Alexander Burnes, to Hyderabad at the amirs' request. The amirs hoped to conclude an offensive-defensive alliance with the British directed against Ranjit Singh whose pretensions to Shikarpur, jointly owned with the amirs of Upper Sind and some forty miles northwest of Khairpur, they had good cause to fear. Of course both Pottinger and Burnes were well aware of the impossibility of concluding such an arrangement, but they hoped to make use of the negotiations to obtain the amirs' permission for a survey of the Indus. Later in the year Nur Mahomed, the principal amir, requested the services of a physician, and Pottinger promptly sent Dr. Hathorn of the 15th Regiment in Cutch to minister to the indisposed prince. But the Bombay Government, although it no longer had any jurisdiction over Sind affairs, which since 1809 had been under direct control of the Central Government,[1] decided to send a doctor itself, whose main duty would be to obtain the concession for which Burnes was already negotiating. The new physician, J. F. Heddle, was sent to Sind on a steam vessel commanded by Lieutenant Carless, who was to survey the Indus on the journey and to remain moored off Hyderabad as long as possible so as to complete the task.

Pottinger was outraged. He ordered Burnes to conduct his affairs without reference to Heddle, although the latter had been told to defer to Burnes in all political matters.[2] With Pottinger's approval, Burnes sent Carless back, as he opposed the mixing of the medical and political missions.[3] Not unnaturally Nur Mahomed did not understand the reason for Heddle's visit, as he was perfectly satisfied with Dr. Hathorn. He treated Heddle courteously but refused to consult him concerning his medical problems, and the doctor, choosing to be insulted, left Hyderabad forthwith.

The Bombay Government immediately complained that Carless would have completed the survey of the Indus had not Pottinger interfered, and W. H. Nathan, the Bombay secretary, when writing to Macnaghten claimed that Heddle had been abused because the amirs knew of Pottinger's feelings and acted from "love or fear of Colonel Pottinger." [4] Consequently when Nur Mahomed sent some presents to Bombay, his envoys were coldly received; as the Bombay Government felt it necessary "to testify its displeasure at the ungracious and insulting manner in which a British officer, who had been deputed at the solicitation, and for the benefit, of one of the Ameers was received by their Highnesses." [5] But the Governor-General agreed with Pottinger that the Bombay Government's interference in the affairs of Sind was unwarranted. Thus Pottinger was soon able to inform Nur Mahomed that his presents to Bombay had been received (a fact he had been able to determine upon seeing them offered for sale in the government gazette), and the amirs in turn agreed to permit a survey of the mouths of the Indus and later of the river itself.

One positive result of Heddle's journey to Hyderabad was his memoir on the River Indus—the most judicious work on the subject written up to that time. He pointed out that the amirs were not guilty of discouraging transit commerce, as had always been supposed. Rather the small volume of trade was due to the extended period of political unrest in the territories along the course of the river. Alterations in the river channel rather than nefarious obstruction by the amirs provided the obstacles to the navigation of the Indus.[6] The subsequent survey of the river conducted by Lieutenants Carless and Wood confirmed this and finally showed the limitations of the Indus as an avenue of commerce, but it did little to dampen the enthusiasm of Lord Auckland, who had succeeded Bentinck as Governor-General. Macnaghten wrote to Bombay:

I am desired to acquaint you that the Governor-General in Council regrets the unfavorable accounts already received regarding the capabilities of the Indus for purposes of commerce but in the opinion of His Lordship in Council it would be premature to record any opinion upon the question at present.[7]

Despite the pessimistic reports Auckland sent an experimental steamer up the Indus and asked the Court to send two or three more steam vessels.[8] He wrote to Sir James Carnac, Governor of Bombay, that the authorities at Bombay were needlessly discouraged by the report of Carless and Wood; and he hoped to encourage trade on the river by the establishment of entrepôts and annual fairs on its banks. With a view to these objects and that of obtaining general information he proposed to send Captain Alexander Burnes on a mission to Lahore and Kabul.[9]

All commercial enterprises on the Indus were inseparably connected with political events, and the policy of Ranjit Singh toward the British and the riverain states, especially Sind, was consequently of prime importance. In 1809 the British had stopped his advance westward by taking the Cis-Sutlej territories under their protection.[10] Ranjit Singh now could expand only in the direction of Sind, and his efficient army commanded by French officers remained an implicit threat to British influence in that area. In 1818 he annexed Multan and in 1823 he advanced as far as Sultan Shahi, sending Generals Allard and Ventura to Mithankot on the pretext that some Baluchis had made an attack on Sikh troops near Multan; but British pressure forced him to withdraw. Between 1825 and 1830 Ranjit Singh undoubtedly could have acquired a part of Sind, as the Company was preoccupied elsewhere. He probably recognized this fact in 1826, when he demanded the payment of tribute from the amirs of Sind on the grounds of having inherited most of the disintegrated Afghan empire and hence a right to the tribute formerly paid by the amirs to Kabul.[11] But Ranjit Singh could not press the issue because of a danger in his rear, in Peshawar, where the fanatic Syed Ahmed had risen in revolt. This threat was not removed until 1831 when Syed Ahmed was killed. In the meantime the British interest had again shifted to the Indus, whose lower reaches they felt must be kept out of Ranjit Singh's hands to insure the success of their commercial enterprises.

Burnes's instructions were to seek permission for a further survey of the Indus and the establishment of a native agent at the mouths of the river. He was also to investigate possible sites for an entrepôt, and annual fair and coaling stations.[12] Auckland wrote:

I am unwilling to give the alarming color of political speculation to a mission, the main object of which is commercial, but it is impossible to divest of political interest any observation of the Countries on the Indus and to the West of the river. It is difficult to see without some anxiety the exertions made on every occasion by the ruler of the Panjab to extend his power; all information from that quarter must be valuable, and it may not be useless ostensibly to mark that nothing which is there passing is viewed with indifference by the British Government or escapes its notice.[13]

BRITISH PREPONDERANCE

Only one man dissented from the general opinion that it was necessary for the security of British India that Sind be preserved as a buffer state and that Ranjit Singh be stopped from making any advances into the area: again, Charles Metcalfe. He said that under the treaty of 1809 the British had no right to interfere with Ranjit's advance on Sind. A war with Lahore might end in the defeat of the British, and even if it resulted in victory for the Company, it would remove a useful buffer between India and Russia. He felt that the Sikhs would be good neighbors and that if it ever became desirable to seize the whole of the Indus river system, the British would have to defeat only one rather than two opponents.[14]

Affairs came to a head in late 1835 when the Sikh armies moved against the Mazaris, a predatory tribe dependent on Sind, who lived a few miles southwest of Mithankot in the no-man's land between the Punjab and Sind. Their capital was Rojhan, and under their chief Behram Khan they lived in a semibarbarous state in reed huts covered by horse blankets. They often raided territories belonging to Lahore, and it was on this pretext that Ranjit Singh decided not only to punish the Mazaris but also the amirs of Sind, under whose jurisdiction they lived. His real aim was no doubt Shikarpur, the important commercial city near the Sikh border.

Ranjit Singh ordered Kanwar Naunihal Singh to proceed to Multan and from there to Mithankot to inform the amirs that if they did not pay the tribute formerly rendered to Kabul, Shikarpur would be occupied. The amirs refused, and the Sikhs occupied Rojhan. They compelled Behram Khan to indemnify them for their losses and to promise to behave better in the future. The amirs now sent envoys to Divan Sanwanmal, the Governor of Multan, and engaged themselves to be responsible for any Sikh losses if Ranjit Singh would only withdraw his forces, which in time he did. But the depredations of the Mazaris did not cease, and in August, 1836, the Sikh troops were once more on the march toward Sind. Divan Sanwanmal again captured Rojhan and carried by assault a small Sindian fort near Shikarpur. To equip his troops Ranjit Singh asked the British for "50,000 stand of arms," but they were refused him.[15] The Governor-General was seriously worried by the Sikh advance, and consequently Macnaghten wrote to Captain C. M. Wade, the British agent in the Punjab:

His Lordship in Council entertains the conviction that the Government of India is bound by the strongest considerations of political interest to prevent the extension of the Sikh power along the whole course of the Indus. It cannot also view with indifference any disturbance of the existing relations of peace between the several states occupying the banks of the river.[16]

When the amirs in desperation asked for British aid against the Sikhs, it conformed with British policy to acquiesce. But the amirs would have to pay a high price for what they received. Pottinger was authorized "to offer our protection against the Sikhs," because the Governor-General hoped

that with a view to enable us to fulfill this obligation, the Ameers would consent permanently to receive and pay the expense of a Body of British Troops to be stationed at their capital. Short of this . . . [Pottinger] was at liberty to offer the mediation of the British Government with Maharaja Ranjeet Singh on condition of the reception of a British Agent at Hyderabad and of course of all relations between Sinde and Lahore being conducted solely through the medium of British officers and at the expense of any temporary deputation of the British troops into Sinde which might be found requisite being defrayed by the Ameers.[17]

Pottinger was also empowered to receive overtures from the amirs for the complete dependence of Sind on Britain, which would require a permanent detachment of British troops in Sind but would guarantee the amirs protection against all enemies.[18]

Wade, at Lahore, was to discuss the matter personally with Ranjit Singh. He was to use every means short of actual threats to keep His Highness at Lahore and to prevent the further advance of his army.[19] If Ranjit Singh attacked anyway, Wade was to remove the Company officers serving with the Sikh army. He was authorized to tell Ranjit Singh that the amirs had placed themselves under British protection but that the British Government was "ready to interpose its good offices for an equitable settlement."[20] The Secret Committee felt that if Ranjit Singh could extend his frontiers appreciably, "his position would require on our part an increase in military force which would be ruinous to our embarrassed finances."[21] They thought that the Indus and its tributary streams should not belong to one state: "The division of power on the Indus between the Scindians, the Afghans and the Sikhs is probably the arrangement most calculated to secure us against hostile use of that River."[22]

Ranjit Singh was forced to yield but continued to occupy much of the Mazari territory and to insist that Shikarpur was beyond the Sutlej, the boundary river in the treaty of 1809.[23] To which Macnaghten replied:

It would appear that the Maharaja regards the British Government as having restricted [by the treaty of 1809] its relations to the countries south of the Sutlej, whereas in point of fact nothing more was stipulated in the treaty referred to as regards the British Government, than it should have no concern with the countries to the north of the river. Of countries to the westward of the Indus no mention was made, and it cannot be admitted for a moment that the treaty had reference to those countries.[24]

Khera points out that legally the British view was incorrect for if north of the Sutlej did not mean west of the Indus, it might as well mean west of the Jhelum or any other river running on the right side of the Sutlej. If this were followed to a logical conclusion, the British could interfere even west of the Jhelum and thus nullify the whole treaty.[25]

While discouraging Ranjit Singh's pretensions to Sind, the British never lost sight of the fact that he was an old and powerful ally. Thus Wade was ordered "to bear in mind that His Lordship in Council considers it of the first importance that you should personally confer with Ranjit Singh and convince him of the disinterested and friendly views of the British Government." [26] Ranjit Singh finally agreed to keep his relations with Sind on the old basis and to destroy the fort his forces had built at Ken in the Mazari country, but he intended to continue the occupation of Rojhan and the Mazari territory.[27]

Auckland feared that the advantages resulting from the free navigation of the Indus had been exposed to imminent hazard by hostilities between the powers occupying the banks of the river, and wrote to the Secret Committee:

Your Honourable Committee will perceive that our negotiation is now narrowed to two objects—the improvement of our relations with the Ameers of Sinde by stationing a British agent at their capital, and the adjustment, with the consent of both parties of the present differences of the Ameers and the Ranjeet Singh—Should these objects be attained, of which there is every possibility, the preservation of tranquility along the whole course of the Indus will be the natural consequence.[28]

In view of the first of these objectives, Pottinger, who arrived in Hyderabad in November, 1836, was soon able to report to the Central Government that he had entered into a provisional agreement with Nur Mahomed providing for the residency of a British agent in Shikarpur.[29] As for Ranjit Singh, although agreeing to a settlement of his dispute with Sind and in time mellowing his stand in regard to Rojhan, he nevertheless informed Wade that he did not immediately wish to drop his claims on Shikarpur or to abandon the Mazari territory as this would cause him to lose face.[30] The British Indian Government was not disposed to press for withdrawal, and Wade was ordered not to insist upon the final abandonment of Ranjit Singh's claims on Shikarpur nor to urge any precipitate settlement with Sind over the Mazari territory.[31]

Both Pottinger and Wade had begun to identify themselves with the views of the government to which they were deputed. Wade supported Ranjit Singh's pretensions to the Mazari territory; while Pottinger wrote:

Our Paramountcy not only entitles, but calls on [us] to stand forward to save the country of Sinde from the aggressions of Ranjeet Singh, and further, that we must establish a decided Political ascendency . . . [and] that the Maharaja should be distinctly warned off.[32]

When Lieutenant Mackeson, Wade's assistant, was appointed to arbitrate between the amirs and the Sikhs on the Mazari question, Pottinger objected because he felt that Mackeson would be prejudiced in favor of Ranjit Singh.[33]

In March, Sir John Keane, the commander in chief, visited Ranjit Singh, and Auckland informed the Secret Committee that the maharajah had consented to withdraw his troops from the Sind frontier. He was willing to accept British arbitration on the Mazari question and would adhere to any agreements made with the Governor-General in an anticipated meeting.[34] Auckland hastened to point out that British mediation was to be on an informal level so as not to bind the Government in any way.[35] Macnaghten wrote to Pottinger: "His Lordship in Council trusts that you will have been specially careful on this point to avoid anything which can be construed as pledging the British Government to a formal and authoritative mediation between the two states."[36]

While the Anglo-Sikh negotiations were still in progress, Burnes had started on his journey north. He again received a hearty welcome at Shikarpur from Rustam, who, now that

Murad Ali, the former Lower Sind *rais*, was dead, wanted an agreement with the British independent of Hyderabad. Burnes "politely but firmly discouraged this wish," as it was no longer felt necessary or desirable to play off Khairpur against Hyderabad.[37] Pottinger reported that the amirs desired provisions for British protection in the new treaty.[38] But Macnaghten replied:

It is not in the policy of the Government by promises of general arbitration and an absolute guarantee of protection, to be implicated without reserve in the uncertain policy and conduct of Sinde, and in the maintenance of all its existing Frontiers, variously acquired as they have been, and wild and ill-controlled as, in many parts, they are.[39]

What he really meant was that any British aid to the amirs was to be inseparably connected with the establishment of a residency in Sind.

The greatest opposition to the treaty came from Mir Sobdar Khan, cousin of Nur Mahomed and son of the senior of the *Char Yar*, Mir Fatehali Khan. He was reported to be quite irreconcilable and to have accused Nur Mahomed of handing over Sind to the *ferengees* (foreigners).[40] The main stumbling block to the treaty, other than the intransigence of Sobdar and some of the Baluchis, was the desire of the amirs that the treaty provide for the British protection of Sind "from Subzulcote this side, and Shikarpoor on that side of the river, down to the sea." [41] But the withdrawal of British troops from Parkur, long a wish of the amirs, seemed to break the back of the opposition, and the amirs, including Sobdar, agreed to the establishment of a British residency.

Pottinger now sent Macnaghten his proposed draft of the treaty, but the latter felt that it was still too binding on the British as they were not willing to promise successful general arbitration with the Sikhs or to offer the amirs protection. "It should be sufficient," he wrote, "that, in support of the agreement as offered by his Lordship in Council, you point out to the Amirs the friendly disposition which has already been pursued towards them." [42] Pottinger replied:

The tenor of all my communications with Noor Mahomed Khan, whether direct or otherwise, has been such as to cause His Highness to understand distinctly that our mediation is dependent on the pleasure and concurrence of the two states (Lahore and Sinde) and that nothing authoritative in it is, or has been contemplated by the Governor-General of India in Council. I have also further repeatedly intimated to the Ameer, that His Lordship's even consenting to undertake the Office of Mediator rests on a British Minister being previously stationed at Hyderabad.[43]

In June, 1837, Pottinger received a treaty draft from the amirs which again stipulated British protection in return for the granting of the residency. Shocked, Auckland wrote:

The proposals now made by His Highness were so different from what we had been led to anticipate, and so totally at variance with the spirit and form of the agreement which Colonel Pottinger had been directed to propose, that he addressed a letter to the Ameer expressing his surprise at the tone of His Highness' present comunication.[44]

A new danger suddenly threatened the final conclusion of the treaty. The Sikhs and the Sindians started negotiations on their own, whose successful culmination would have obviated the need for British arbitration and hence the necessity for the amirs to accept a British resident. As Ranjit Singh in the terms demanded a token tribute of horses and other articles, Macnaghten informed Wade: "the British desire for peace on the Indus necessitated it not becoming party to any terms which would subvert the independence of any state with which the British Government was in friendly alliance." [45]

BRITISH PREPONDERANCE

To Pottinger he wrote:

In communicating to their Highness the intelligence adverted to in the correspondence with Captain Wade, you will state that though the Governor-General in Council could not but rejoice at the establishment without his intervention of friendly relations between their Highnesses and Maharaja Ranjit Singh on the basis of mutual independence, yet it must be obvious to the Ameers that any favorable terms which they may gain must be owing in a great measure to the friendly interest in the welfare of the Sinde state expressed by the British Government, and the opportunity might be taken of distinctly declaring that if they continue to manifest so great an aversion to form a closer alliance with the only power competent to render them efficient aid, the British Government must refrain on any future occasion to secure their independence.[46]

Fortunately, from the British point of view, the negotiations between Ranjit Singh and the amirs of Sind collapsed, and the Governor-General was able to order Pottinger to inform the amirs that unless the residency was conceded "the British Government could not exert its influence or use its good offices with Maharajah Ranjeet Singh for the restoration of the Mazari Districts and the abandonment of his designs against Sind." [47]

The amirs, having no alternative, finally agreed to the treaty; and on April 23, 1838, Auckland reported to the Secret Committee that an agreement had been signed with the amirs of Hyderabad whereby a British resident was to be stationed at Hyderabad, the British were to use their good offices for the settlement of Sikh-Sind conflict, and all intercourse between the Sikhs and Lahore was in future to be conducted through the medium of the British Government. Separate documents were granted to the junior amirs, but Nur Mahomed in association with his brother, Nasir Khan, was recognized as the chief

41

BRITISH PREPONDERANCE

with whom alone the British would deal. Colonel Pottinger was appointed resident and Captain P. M. Melvill, of the 7th Regiment of the Bombay Native Infantry, was named his assistant and British agent for the navigation of the lower course of the Indus.[48]

4. The Afghan Crisis
(1838–1841)

BRITISH FEAR of a Russian invasion through one of the northwestern states was probably the single most important determinant of policy toward that region in the first half of the nineteenth century. The area was hardly ever free of turmoil, and with the settlement of the Sikh-Sind crisis, the Afghan-Sikh difficulties now assumed serious proportions. Ranjit Singh had seized Peshawar in 1835 upon Shah Shuja's last attempt to regain his throne, and Afghan policy ever since had been directed toward its recovery. In early 1837 the Governor-General was "satisfied that there is yet no adequate motive for the interposition of the British power in the contests of the Sikhs and the Afghans," and he did not anticipate any greater result from Alexander Burnes's mission to Kabul than "the collection of accurate information, the extension of commercial intercourse and the conciliation of friendly sentiments." [1] In August, however, Wade wrote Macnaghten that the Afghans were contemplating an alliance with Persia in order to achieve their aims against the Sikhs. This intelligence put a new complexion on things, and Wade suggested that the British should offer to mediate between Dost Mahomed and Ranjit Singh. If Dost Mahomed refused to coöperate, the British should work with the Sikhs and Sindians against the Afghans.[2] Auckland himself felt that events had changed the nature of Burnes's journey from a purely commercial and good-will venture into a political and diplomatic mission to counteract the designs of Russia and Persia.[3]

43

THE AFGHAN CRISIS

Burnes arrived in Kabul on September 20, 1837, and was received by Dost Mahomed "with most gratifying demonstrations of respect and civility." [4] But he soon reported to Auckland that the Afghan ruler showed a marked predilection for the Russians and Persians.[5] Actually Dost Mahomed had frequently indicated his preference of a British connection to one with Russia,[6] but British failure to support his designs on Peshawar led him to look elsewhere for aid. The danger to India no doubt was greatly exaggerated, but the combination of the Russophobe Palmerston at the Foreign Office and the activities of the Russian agents, Simonitch in Persia and Vikovitch in Kabul, caused Auckland seriously to consider active intervention in the affairs of Afghanistan, although he had started his administration as a confirmed opponent of territorial aggrandizement. When the Persians at the Russian behest invaded western Afghanistan and besieged Herat (which was not under Kabul's jurisdiction), Auckland decided to replace Dost Mahomed with a ruler more friendly to British designs in Central Asia. The candidate of his choice was the oft defeated but ever hopeful former monarch, Shah Shuja-ul-Mulk, whose aspirations the British had previously often spurned. Auckland wrote:

As to the justice of the course about to be pursued there cannot exist a reasonable doubt. We owe it to our safety to assist the lawful sovereign of Afghanistan in the recovery of his throne. The welfare of our possessions in the East requires that we should in the present crisis of affairs have a decidedly friendly power on our frontier and that we should have an ally who is interested in resisting aggression and establishing tranquility in place of a Chief seeking to identify himself with those whose schemes of aggrandizement and conquest are not to be disguised.[7]

Once again unrest on the borders of the empire was demanding direct intervention in countries which the British had no interest in acquiring.

THE AFGHAN CRISIS

The Secret Committee approved of Auckland's action, but assumed that

you have not only had certain proofs that those chieftains were irretrievably committed to a policy hostile to British interests—but, also, that you had the full persuasion that the restoration of Shah Shujah would be acceptable to the great body of Afghans, and moreover that he might be maintained upon the throne more by his own influence and the justice of his sway than by the continued manifest interference of the British government.[8]

This assumption was illusory. The failure of Shah Shuja's many previous attempts to regain his throne paid eloquent testimony to his unpopularity with the Afghan chiefs and their subjects. Former Governors-General had been aware of this, and Bentinck, when Shuja had applied to him for support in his 1834 invasion of Afghanistan, had written: "This Government though it did not feel justified in prohibiting the movement of Shah Shooja, had invariably refused to afford him the assistance which he had repeatedly solicited, in aid of his undertaking."[9] Later, in 1836, the former king was threatened with expulsion from Ludhiana if he ever again attempted to replace Dost Mahomed.[10]

But Auckland, influenced by a misguided Macnaghten and a misleading Burnes, determined to persevere. To achieve the replacement of Dost Mahomed with Shah Shuja it was necessary to gain the coöperation of Ranjit Singh and to acquire the right of transit through Sind as well as certain further concessions from the amirs. It was decided that to defray some of the expenses of the expedition and to assure funds to reward Ranjit Singh for his coöperation, the fiction of a tribute payable to Shah Shuja as suzerain of the amirs of Sind would be revived; and a treaty to this effect was signed by the British, Shah Shuja, and Ranjit Singh without the amirs even being a party to it.

45

The tripartite treaty of June, 1838, set up the machinery for the invasion of Afghanistan. The sixteenth article provided that Shah Shuja would relinquish all claims on the amirs of Sind for a sum to be determined by the British, and it was anticipated that the amount would be in excess of twenty lakhs.[11]

The Ameers must be made sensible that if they should now deprive themselves of the advantage of his Lordship's mediation . . . the British Government will be precluded from offering opposition to any measures for the assertion of those claims which the Shah may eventually determine to adopt.[12]

The resident was to inform the amirs that Bombay troops might have to occupy Shikarpur in the present emergency and that the article of the former treaty which prohibited the passage of military stores up the Indus would of necessity have to be suspended.[13]

Auckland now clearly needed a pretext for exacting a new treaty from the amirs which so thoroughly reversed the provisions of previous agreements. Fortunately for him, on August 13, 1838, Pottinger wrote to Macnaghten that the principal amirs of Hyderabad had written a letter to the Shah of Persia. Pottinger himself did not attach much importance to this as all amirs except Sobdar (who was a Sunni and had not joined in the writing of the letter) were Shias and hence considered the Shah their ecclesiastical superior.[14] Auckland immediately seized upon this correspondence. He wrote: "The Ameers of Sinde though all professing friendship have some of them been corresponding in terms of submission . . . with the Persians, and would thereby justify any course which we may think it expedient to adopt towards them." [15] He later concluded, "The Ameers spoke fairly but acted foully." [16] Pottinger was ordered to take the strongest action against Nur Mahomed "for his duplicity in making at the same moment profession of submission to Persia and of close alliance with the British Government." [17] If only Sobdar was loyal, it should be investigated

THE AFGHAN CRISIS

whether he should not be put at the head of the Sind Government. "Those who are not our friends on the day of trial will be considered our enemies," the Governor-General wrote, "and unhappily it is amongst those that Nur Mahomed has apparently chosen to rank himself." [18] At this juncture the Persians besieging Herat withdrew their forces, leaving Auckland a perfect opportunity to extricate himself from what had the makings of a most embarrassing situation. But urged on by the ambitious Macnaghten, he persisted in his course.

The Indus Valley and the Bolan Pass were chosen as the main path into Afghanistan rather than the more desirable Khyber Pass, which Ranjit Singh controlled and transit through which he discouraged. Thus when the amirs refused Shuja's demand for passage through their territories, the Governor-General wrote:

The treachery of the Ameers is fully established by a variety of concurrent circumstances, of their having written a slavish areeza to the Shah of Persia . . . by the treatment openly shown to a self-styled Persian Prince at Hyderabad and their insulting letter to Shah Shoojah ool Moolk coupled with the distinct announcement . . . regarding opposition to the Shah.[19]

As it turned out, none of these accusations could be substantiated. Nevertheless, Auckland decided to station a subsidiary force in Sind [20] and if necessary not only to elevate Sobdar to the chieftainship but to guarantee each amir in his separate possessions in return for payment of a share of the subsidy which the Governor-General intended to charge for the maintenance of the British troops in Sind. "By separating the territorial interest of each chief, a separation of their interests will probably follow," [21] making it easier to collect the subsidy.

Pottinger had not progressed very far in his negotiations when the amirs produced releases from all tribute payments, which Shah Shuja had signed in 1835 in return for aid the amirs had rendered him in his abortive invasion of Afghanistan. Shuja

47

THE AFGHAN CRISIS

had agreed to "bestow Sind and Shikarpur and their dependencies on you and your heirs and successors in the same manner that you now hold them. They shall be your territories and property." [22] The documents were obviously genuine, but when Pottinger duly reported this fact to Auckland, Macnaghten replied:

The Governor-General refrains for the present from recording any opinion relative to the releases which His Majesty Shah Sooja is stated to have executed. Admitting the documents produced to be genuine, and that they imply a relinquishment of all claim to tribute, still they would hardly appear to be applicable to the present circumstances, and it is not conceivable, that His Majesty should have foregone so valuable a claim, without some equivalent, or that some counterpart agreement should not have been taken, the non-fulfillment of the terms of which, may have rendered null and void, His Majesty's Engagements.[23]

With such fatuous reasoning the Governor-General dismissed the amirs' claims.

Auckland summarized the British objects in Sind as being "the relief of the navigation of the Indus from all toll, the maintenance of a local British Force, and the separate independence of each chief." [24] Pottinger had meanwhile gained the reluctant consent of Nur Mahomed for the passage of British troops through Sind and had deputed Lieutenant W. J. Eastwick to conduct the negotiations on his behalf in Hyderabad. He instructed Eastwick to excuse Sobdar, because of his friendly behavior, from the payment of any subsidy. Should the amirs ask what was to prevent the British from demanding even more once they had submitted to the present terms, Eastwick was to reply that it was

the strong instance of our good faith and the wish to preserve our amicable relations as exemplified in the treaty you convey to them. . . . We render them our renewed friendship and

48

protection on such moderate terms, and accompanied by so many advantages, that their refusal of the former will show to the world their resolution not to meet us half-way, and to oblige us to take by force, what we ask as friends and protectors.[25]

The abolition of the Indus toll, Pottinger pointed out, would cost the amirs only about Rs. 2,000–3,000 and would be more than repaid by the thousands of merchants who would then flock to Sind to sell their goods. As to the bringing of troops into the country, "they have only themselves to thank for rendering the arrangement imperative. Had they all acted with the good faith and fidelity we have observed towards them, no such measure could have been thought necessary." [26] Not only had the amirs refused to aid Shuja but they had talked of calling in the Persians, the enemies of the British, to aid them. Eastwick was to take the earliest opportunity of intimating to all the amirs "that the smallest act of hostility will plunge matters beyond the chance of recall." [27]

Eastwick, accompanied by Captain Outram and Lieutenant Leckie, arrived in Hyderabad in January, 1839. He carried with him a draft of the proposed new treaty of twenty-three articles. The deputation soon had an audience with the amirs. Nur Mahomed produced a box from which he took, one by one, all the past treaties with the British. He then asked:

What is to become of all these? Since the day that Sind has been connected with the English there has always been something new; your government is never satisfied; we are anxious for your friendship but we cannot be continually persecuted. We have given a road to your troops through our territories and now you wish to remain. This the Baloochees will never suffer. But still we might arrange this matter, were we certain that we should not be harassed with other demands.[28]

He asked about the subsidy to Shuja, which matter had been left in abeyance for more than four months. "Is this a proof of

THE AFGHAN CRISIS

friendship?" he wanted to know. "We have failed in nothing; we have furnished camels, boats, grains; we have distressed ourselves to supply your wants."[29]

Among the provisions of the proposed treaty the amirs particularly objected to Article 13 which would allow the British to use Karachi when weather conditions made the entrance of the mouths of the Indus impassable, to the independence granted to each chief, and to the exemption from the subsidy granted to Mir Sobdar (who after all had been the most vociferous foe of the British in the past and had not been implicated in the letter to the Shah of Persia only because he was a Sunni). As to the subsidy itself, Nur Mahomed's opposition was vociferous. He said: "We ought never to have granted a road through our territories; that was my act alone, all the Baloochees predicted what would happen; this is the consequence of friendship."[30]

Leckie replied:

This is the consequence of a want of friendship you have only to thank yourselves. . . . As to the benefits resulting from the introduction of a British force into Sinde, they were clear and palpable; employment would be given to thousands, a vast influx of capital would encourage commerce and manufactures, this would eventually find its way into the treasuries of their Highnesses. The Indus, now so barren, would teem with vessels, jungle would yield to the plough, and prosperity succeed to decay and depopulation.[31]

Nur Mahomed did not see how all this concerned the amirs:

Our Hunting preserves will be destroyed, our enjoyments curtailed; you tell us that money will find its way into our treasury, it does not appear so, our contractors write to us, that they are bankrupt, they have no means of fulfilling their contracts; boats, camels, are all absorbed by the English troops, trade is at a stand; pestilence has fallen on the land.[32]

50

THE AFGHAN CRISIS

So saying the amirs prepared to resist the British. Sher Mahomed marched into the capital with a body of troops from Mirpur, and Baluchis flocked in from far and wide to defend Hyderabad. But the sight of the Bombay and Bengal divisions converging on the city sapped the amirs' will to resist and they gave in, cheating the army, as Sir John Keane put it, "of a pretty piece of practice."

The Mirs had meanwhile been deprived of Karachi, which the British had long wished to obtain. Admiral Frederick Maitland, while transporting the Bombay reserve force under Brigadier T. Valiant, claimed he was fired on by the Fort of Manora. He promptly bombarded it and captured the town. Sometime later Pottinger, who could hardly be called a partisan of the amirs, wrote the following reports in which he did not hesitate to avow his conviction that the whole procedure could have been advantageously avoided. He stated that the only shot fired as the admiral approached was the salute customary when a square-rigged vessel came in sight or approached the place: "This I had myself witnessed when I came to the Port in 1809 with the mission under Mr. Smith, and I likewise know it was done when His Majesty's Frigate Challenger anchored off it in 1830." [33] It was also the custom at the lighthouse at Bombay. The amirs in an interview with Pottinger declared that there had been no shot in the cannon at the time it was fired and he, in later investigations, determined that there was not a single ball in the fort that would fit any of the guns and that the whole supply of gunpowder amounted to six pounds which was kept in an earthen pot. The entire garrison consisting of sixteen men, many of whom were armed only with swords, were standing outside the fort admiring the *Wellesley* when the firing began. The Governor of Karachi informed Pottinger that rather than resisting the landing, he had orders from the amirs to coöperate with the British in every way.[34]

Pottinger objected to the seizure of Karachi. He felt that the British should be allowed free access to the port but that it should be returned to the amirs. He also thought that the Governor-General should obtain a release for Shikarpur from Shuja to show the amirs "that we do not lose sight of their interests." [35]

As for the amirs, they continued to make certain demands: that the British relinquish Karachi and that the cantonments in the Karachi and Hyderabad areas be some distance from the town, that the number of British troops to be quartered in Sind be defined, and that the 3,000 Sindian troops provided for in the draft treaty should never be forced to go beyond the Sind frontier; that the British should not interfere in internal disputes; that the towns included in the treaty be specifically named, and that the Hyderabad rupee should be the medium of exchange in all tribute and subsidy payments rather than the Company rupee, which was more valuable.[36] Pottinger himself urged the use of the Hyderabad rupee, because the use of the Company rupee would press too hard on the amirs' financial resources, which he had overestimated.[37] But the Governor-General rejected Pottinger's suggestions. He considered that the amirs were not being assessed very heavily, as the British were bearing most of the expenses. Auckland also declined to be more specific in regard to places included in the treaty. Each amir was now to be treated as a separate entity and Auckland had no intimate knowledge of the possessions of each. The stipulation concerning the Sind troops, he stated, was included mainly as a symbol of Sind's subordinate position, and the Governor-General would not limit the amirs' obligation by permitting these troops to serve only in Sind. The question of Shikarpur was to be turned over to Shuja and the Governor-General's envoy to the Afghan pretender, William Macnaghten.[38] In regard to Karachi

the Governor-General will not call into question the correctness of the reports from the Naval Commander in Chief from which it appears no attention was payed to his pacific overtures before he felt himself compelled to resort to force, nor will his Lordship

THE AFGHAN CRISIS

admit the denial by the Ameers or their subjects of a hostile spirit having swayed their conduct at Karachee or elsewhere. The conduct evinced to the British mission at Hyderabad, the preparations for resistance at the Capital, the intrigues in which they were engaged with our enemies and their procrastination in submitting to the terms of our treaty are all convincing proofs of the faithless and unfriendly spirit of the Ameers and ought not to now be an argument for further concession.[39]

The amirs of Hyderabad were meanwhile mulcted of twenty lakhs of rupees for the payment of Shah Shuja, ten of which were paid at the time of the acceptance of the draft treaty.[40]

The final form of the treaty as sent from Calcutta by Auckland consisted of 14 articles and was more stringent than Pottinger's draft of 23 articles. It provided for a British force to be stationed in Sind, at Tatta or such other place westward of the Indus as the Governor-General might select. The strength of this force would also be determined by the Governor-General but would not exceed 5,000 men. Mirs Nur Mahomed Khan, Nasir Mahomed Khan, and Mir Mahomed Khan were to pay one lakh of company rupees annually, making a total of three lakhs per annum for support of the British force. Mir Sobdar was exempt from any payment. The British Government took upon itself the protection of the territories possessed by the amirs of Hyderabad, and the four amirs were guaranteed in their holdings, but as separate entities. The British agent would mediate in any conflict between the various amirs and if necessary aid the aggrieved party. The amirs could not enter into negotiation with any foreign chief or state without the knowledge and sanction of the British Government. They would supply, when required, 3,000 men both foot and horse, to work in "subordinate cooperation" with the British for purposes of defense, and the British would pay these troops when they were serving beyond the Sind frontier. The Bakroo or Timooree rupee current in Sind was declared to be of equal value with the Company rupee, and the British could set up a mint in Sind for the coining of the

THE AFGHAN CRISIS

Bakroo or Timooree rupee, but would have to pay the amirs seigniorage after the conclusion of the Afghan war. No toll was to be levied on ships passing up and down the Indus within the territories of the Amirs of Sind, but any goods landed were subject to the usual duties of the country; of course goods to be sold in a British cantonment would be exempt from such duties.[41] The treaty was ratified by the Governor-General in March, 1839, and Karachi was provided for in a separate agreement drawn up at the time of its capture between Rear Admiral Frederick Lewis Maitland and Brigadier T. Valiant on the part of the British and Hassal Ben Butcha, the commandant of Manora Fort, and Khyer Mahomed, the Governor of Karachi, on behalf of Nur Mahomed. The first article was the most significant; it said simply "that the full possession of the fort and town of Kurrachee shall be this day given up by the aforesaid Governor to the British forces." The occupation was originally intended to be temporary and the civil government was to be continued "by the authorities of the place" [42] but the amirs of Sind were destined never to recover Karachi.

To complement Eastwick's negotiations at Hyderabad, Lieutenant Colonel Sir Alexander Burnes, newly returned from his unsuccessful mission to Kabul, was deputed to Khairpur to conclude a treaty with Mir Rustam Khan, as British policy had again reverted to encouraging the independence of Khairpur from Hyderabad. He was welcomed by the old chief, who, when informed of the approach of Sir Henry Fane, declared his great satisfaction and said he himself would go to Rohri "that he might show every mark of respect to a person of his Excellency's high rank, and contribute, as far as he could, to the comfort of his voyage and passage through Sinde." [43] Burnes asked Rustam to allow the British to occupy the prime defensive position of Bukkur and the Amir replied that

in giving up Bukkur to the British, he had to encounter great disgrace; that his tribe and family were alike opposed to it; but

54

THE AFGHAN CRISIS

that he was an old man, with but a few years to live, and it was to save his children and his tribe from ruin that he had years ago resolved on allying himself to us; that other invaders of India might be resisted, but if one of our armies were swept away, we could send another, and that such power induced him alike to fear and rely upon us; that he was henceforward the submissive and obedient servant of the British.[44]

The treaty drawn up between Burnes and Rustam on December 24, 1838, provided for perpetual friendship between Mir Rustam, his heirs and successors, and the British Government. The British for their part engaged to protect the principality and territory of Khairpur. Mir Rustam and his heirs acknowledged the supremacy of the British Government and bound themselves to work in subordinate coöperation with it and to have no connection with any other chief or state. The Amir was to commit no aggression and the British Government would arbitrate any dispute which arose. He would furnish troops according to his means, render all possible aid and assistance to the British during the course of the Afghan war, and would approve of all defensive preparations which the British might deem necessary. A British resident with an appropriate escort was to be stationed in Khairpur.[45] A separate article provided that the Company could occupy the island of Bukkur in time of war.[46] Rustam was also excused from paying anything in support of the Company troops, but the British intended to force Rustam's brother Mir Mubarak Khan to pay a subsidy, as he had been the chief opponent of the British in Khairpur. Rustam, however, insisted that Mubarak receive the same treatment as himself, and an agreement was drawn up to this effect not only with Mubarak but with Mirs Mahomed Khan and Mahomed Ali Khan.[47] Auckland, however, evaded the spirit of the agreement. He did not charge Mubarak anything for the support of British troops in Sind but he determined to collect from him the seven lakhs of

55

THE AFGHAN CRISIS

rupees which was the Khairpur share of the sum payable to Shah Shuja—or at least as much of the money as Mubarak's resources would permit.[48]

The treaty structure was completed in July, 1841, when an agreement was signed with Sher Mahomed of Mirpur after the settlement of the long-standing land dispute between the Mirpur and Hyderabad families. The treaty was similar to the one drawn up with Rustam Khan and provided for the freedom of navigation in the Mirpur section of the Indus. Sher Mahomed had hoped to avoid the payment of a subsidy, but the British made Rs. 50,000 annually the price for guaranteeing him in his possessions.[49] The diplomatic negotiations required by the Afghan war were now concluded. The amirs of Hyderabad were still technically independent but their activities and jurisdiction over their own affairs had been greatly circumscribed while Khairpur was essentially a British protectorate. Auckland wrote to the Secret Committee:

To ourselves it is so desirable to have the military control of the Indus that it would have been highly expedient to introduce our troops into Sinde, even were the whole cost to be payed from our treasuries . . . I may be permitted to offer my congratulations to your Honorable Committee, upon this timely settlement of our relations with Sinde, by which our Political and Military ascendancy in that province is now firmly declared and confirmed. The main provisions of the . . . engagements are that the Confederacy of the Ameers is virtually dissolved, each Chief being upheld in his own possessions and bound to refer his differences with the other chiefs to our arbitration—*that Sinde is placed formally under British protection and brought within the circle of our Indian relations*—that a British Force is to be fixed in Lower Sinde at Tatta or such other point as the British may determine.[50]

Hobhouse, who was about to leave office as chairman of the Board of Control, minuted in the margin: "My successor will

THE AFGHAN CRISIS

of course take immediate notice of this unfortunate arrangement," [51] and the Secret Committee felt that

> the virtual establishment of British authority throughout Sinde may have been justified by the conduct of the Ameers and by the paramount necessity of securing the line of the Indus for purposes of defence as of commercial enterprise. But it is not to be denied that by reducing the Ameers of Sinde to the condition of Tributary and Protected Princes of Hindoostan you have in fact extended the limits of the Indian Empire and may give countenance to the charge of having departed from the resolution proclaimed in your declaration of 1st October, not to attempt any territorial aggrandizement.[52]

After the conclusion of the treaties with Hyderabad and Khairpur, an Upper Sind political agency was added to that of Lower Sind. In January, 1840, Colonel Henry Pottinger, troubled by ill health, and mortified by the rapid rise of his erstwhile subordinate Alexander Burnes and the reliance placed on him by the Governor-General, resigned and was replaced by Captain James Outram. Ross Bell, a Bengal civilian, was placed at the head of the new Upper Sind political agency. Bell was a man of some ability but he was arrogant, officious, and had a personality calculated to grate against those with whom he came in touch. His two principal assistants, Lieutenant Brown at Sukkur and Captain Kennedy at Khairpur, were cut from the same cloth. None of the three was well trained in the languages or customs of the area. Ali Murad, the younger brother of Mir Rustam, was a favorite of Bell; and when a land dispute arose between Ali Murad and Nasir Khan of Khairpur, Bell rendered a decision in favor of the former. This act eventually precipitated a short period of hostilities whose outcome allowed Ali Murad to obtain some villages from Nasir Khan and Rustam under the provisions of the Treaty of Nunahar signed in September of 1842. Bell was inimical to

THE AFGHAN CRISIS

Rustam and particularly to the aged Mir's trusted minister, Fateh Mahomed Ghori.

The great power of the political agent was manifested when Bell differed with Brigadier W. Gordon, the commander of the troops in Upper Sind, over the conduct of his men, and Auckland supported the agent. [53] When Nott advanced on Kelat without first obtaining Bell's permission, the Governor-General expressed his strong disapproval.[54] But the authorities in England were becoming increasingly displeased with Bell. Hobhouse was "exceedingly discontented with the correspondence of Mr. Ross Bell . . . with your Government";[55] while the Secret Committee thought "it highly inexpedient to employ a functionary in so important a station as that of Mr. Bell, with whose conduct, Government is repeatedly compelled to find fault." [56] Auckland agreed

with nearly all who watched his career that his conduct and demeanor towards other officers were such as to repel confidence and cooperation and to impair whatever he might otherwise have of efficiency. . . . We have no officer of greater powers of activity and arrangement than he has, but there are few also of greater defects of character and of temper, and it is very mortifying to me that my many efforts to turn his better parts to account, should have failed.[57]

Outram was consequently ordered to make arrangements to replace Bell and to assume command of both agencies;[58] but before this could be effected, Bell, who had not been in good health, died. Thus, with the combining of the political agencies for Upper and Lower Sind, was born the Sind agency, and a new class of officials, versed in the local language and more knowledgeable about the country than their predeccessors, began to develop.[59]

Despite his policy toward Afghanistan the development of trade on the Indus was perhaps Auckland's chief goal. He wrote: "If I can open channels of commerce to Central Asia and if I

58

THE AFGHAN CRISIS

can make the Indus the thoroughfare for navigation, that gold and silver road (as the Burmese would call it) which it ought to be, I shall not care for much else." [60] He informed Hobhouse that he planned to start a monthly boat service between Bukkur and Tatta, and Bukkur and Ferozepur, as soon as events would allow it.[61] He was determined "that five boats of 300 maunds [about 12½ tons] each shall start from Ferozepore for Bukkur, every fortnight, from the first of June, with passengers and goods." [62] The Governor-General awaited with great interest the first experiment with steam on the Indus. "I look upon the Indus," he wrote, "as the high road from London to Delhi and it requires but good arrangements to make the travelling easy." [63] But Auckland proved to be too optimistic: the Indus steamer could not reach Ferozepur because it could make only six and a half knots and drew three feet of water even with the masts, tanks, and heavy equipment removed. Captain Carless, the vessel's commander looked forward "with anxiety to the accounts of the navigation of the Indus during the next 6 months. If they should be unfavorable he would almost despair of any beneficial navigation of the River." [64] Auckland was not, however, greatly dismayed and proceeded with his plans for the establishment of a great fair on the banks of the Indus, which, it was later decided, would be held at Sukkur in January, 1841. But accounts of the navigation of the Indus continued to be discouraging, and the Governor-General finally gave them some credence;[65] still he wrote to Hobhouse that "not only was the time of year the most unfavorable but the river was lower, than in ordinary seasons at that time of year." [66]

Trouble now arose between the amirs and the British over the charging of tolls at Karachi. The amirs agreed to remove their most recent taxes but claimed that they (especially Nasir Khan) thus would lose a considerable amount annually. Outram thought that it would not be proper to require a further reduction of inland transit duties beyond what was formerly levied, "more than which can not fairly be expected while yet in the

THE AFGHAN CRISIS

infancy of our Indus commerce. No visible advantage has been derived by the Ameers from their mercantile connection with us." [67] But "the evil must soon however correct itself," he continued, "for when traffic by the river has been more fully established, unless the inland transit duties are totally abolished nothing whatever will be carried by land." [68] The Governor-General agreed that the former duties should be maintained but that no additional advantage should be derived from the necessity of supplying the British troops in Karachi. [69]

The whole matter of the Indus tolls was again to become a matter of contention. Although Pottinger had advised Outram to check the amirs' disposition to charge tolls on the river, [70] the problem was not a simple one. The amirs claimed that the treaty of 1832 guaranteed them the right to tax their own subjects, and it must be remembered that Bentinck had urged Pottinger in 1833 to give "the Ameers every assurance that the internal trade of their own country will not be interfered with." [71] Outram indicated several difficulties to the Governor-General. One was how to get Sher Mahomed to stop taxing his own subjects as he was not a party to the recent treaty with Hyderabad. The amirs of Hyderabad, he pointed out, were guaranteed the absolute rule of their respective principalities by the fifth article of the treaty of 1839, and had before them the example of the rulers of Khairpur and Bahawalpur, who were allowed to tax their subjects on the river. The amirs continued to claim that the eleventh and twelfth articles of the treaty of 1839 [72] merely reaffirmed the old commercial treaties of 1832 and 1834 and that the eleventh article referred only to foreign merchants.

Outram himself soon became more sympathetic to the Talpur cause. He realized that Pottinger had written Eastwick on November 29, 1839, that "no customs duties are to be levied on any goods (*no matter who the owners are*) going or coming by the Indus." [73] But he had discovered the inefficiency and dishonesty of the native agent, Jeth Anand, and concluded that the amirs had never been apprized by him of the true nature of Pottinger's demands.[74] Outram believed that it was quite likely that the amirs thought that the eleventh and twelfth articles of the new treaty confirmed the old commercial treaties, especially as the fifth article of the treaty of 1839 provided for the absolute rule of the amirs over their own subjects. It was not plausible, Outram continued, that the amirs would have allowed such a curtailment of their powers without strong remonstrances, especially as they were vehemently opposed to some less important articles. Petamber, the residency *munshi* (clerk), who was present at the treaty negotiations, said they made no such objections. Outram felt that the Company could afford to be lenient as eventually all trade would be driven, by the taxes, to foreign merch ts who were not taxed, and the encouragement of European traders was what had originally been intended. As other states were allowed to tax their subjects on the Indus, the amirs' pride was hurt, and those offended included Mirs Sobdar and Sher Mahomed, the particular friends of the British. When the amirs saw the Europeans prospering they would rescind the taxes. Meanwhile the chief objection to letting the amirs tax their own subjects was the taxing of empty boats, which Outram was sure they would stop if the British were only willing to compromise. Outram concluded his lengthy dispatch by quoting Benjamin Franklin:

To me it seems, that neither the obtaining nor the retaining of any trade—however valuable—is an object for which men may justly spill each others blood, that the true and sure means of extending and securing commerce is the goodness and cheapness of commodities, and the profit of no trade can ever be equal to the expense of compelling it, and of holding it by fleets and armies.[75]

When no answer was immediately forthcoming from Fort William, Outram again pointed out that Jeth Anand had not accurately explained Pottinger's views to the amirs and urged the liberal application of the eleventh article of the treaty of 1839 and also of the twelfth article which provided that any merchandise landed from boats traveling up or down the river should be subject to the usual duty of the country where it was unloaded.[76]

Meanwhile the amirs continued to deny they had ever received orders from Pottinger not to tax any vessels on the Indus. Nur Mahomed, in consternation, exclaimed: "How are we to live? We desire no advantage from foreign commerce, and if what we always got from our subjects is taken away, how can we exist for the taxes on the Sinde boats, and produce is all our revenue." [77]

The Governor-General finally replied that "the Ameers of Hyderabad are not, as a matter of *right* to be considered as being, in respect to duties on the Indus, in any degree in the same position as the Ameers of Khyrpoor or the Nawab of Bhawalpore." [78] Bahawal Khan was allowed to levy tolls under the treaties of 1833 and 1835, although it was hoped that he would allow amendment of these. The Hyderabad amirs had been recalcitrant and hence were not allowed the same right as the rulers of Khairpur and Bahawalpur. The Governor-General suggested that the amirs tax their own subjects on shore, either before embarkation or after debarkation. He felt that if the amirs were allowed to tax the products of Lower Sind merchants traveling on Lower Sind boats, it could not help but interfere with foreign commerce as the goods of foreign merchants would of necessity have to travel on the same boats. As for Sher Mahomed of Mirpur, he had no valid claim to levy taxes on his part of the river. The treaty drawn up between Sher Mahomed and Pottinger was based on the one drawn up previously with the amirs of Hyderabad, the Governor-General stated. One condition of this earlier agreement was that no toll should be levied from the sea upward within the territories of the amirs of Hyderabad:

It could be ill borne that a subordinate chief, who, as you remark, at the date of the agreement, was regarded "as a subject or member of the government of Sinde" should now stand upon his supposed independence, and separating himself from the Ameers, impede and impair the beneficial effects of this great public measure.[79]

Actually Auckland's views contravened many provisions of the various Anglo-Sind treaties, but Hobhouse noted on one of the Governor-General's letters:

Say we consider his Lordship's views on this important subject correct—The Ameers of Lower Sinde ought not to be treated as conquered princes but it must not be forgotten that they opposed, as long as they could with safety, all our operations in the late expedition—and may be considered bound not only by the letter but the spirit of the Treaty of Hyderabad.[80]

While the amirs of Hyderabad remained adamant in defense of their rights, Mir Rustam Khan agreed not to levy any tolls on his part of the river even on his own subjects. But far from being appreciative, the British exhumed the matter of the seven lakhs they had assessed Mubarak as his share of the tribute payable to Shuja. As Mubarak had died in 1839, it was decided that his heirs would have to pay this sum. The Governor-General stated that the guarantee of the integrity of his territories would not apply to Nasir Khan (the son of Mubarak) until he had followed the example of the amirs of Hyderabad in regard to the tribute to Shuja. "It is important that all the chiefs with territory along the banks of the Indus," he wrote, "should be within the operation of this guarantee." [81] The Government felt that the exemption granted to Mubarak by Burnes at Rustam's insistence excused him from the subsidy payable to the British but not from the tribute.

The matter was destined to remain unsettled for some time, but the difficulties in collecting monetary assessments from the amirs prompted the Governor-General to think of commuting the subsidy payments due from the amirs. He proposed, "A cession to the British Government of the lands and revenues of Shikarpore, a measure the present advantages of which should not be lost sight of in the event of any failure on the part of the Ameers in their pecuniary obligation to us." [82] This was not the first time the matter had come up. In 1838 both Nur Mahomed and Nasir Khan of Hyderabad had suggested a cession of part of the revenues of Shikarpur to pay for the expenses of any British troops which might be needed to settle the Sind-Sikh dispute. But the offer had not been pursued by Pottinger. Now the cession of Shikarpur and its arrondissements was considered desirable, as its possession, it was felt, would act as an impetus to commerce by insuring protection and justice to traders. [83] Of the revenue of Shikarpur four-sevenths accrued to Hyderabad, and three-sevenths were collected by Khairpur. Out of this last amount two-thirds belonged to Rustam and one-third to Nasir Khan. Bell had early concluded that "the former could not be requested to cede his right without receiving an Equivalent, although the latter might with advantage be arranged on the subject—as he owes 7 lakhs of rupees to Shah Soojah." [84]

In December, 1841, Nur Mahomed of Hyderabad had died, and his heirs, Nasir Khan and Hussein Ali, were willing to give up their share of Shikarpur on certain specific terms: Shikarpur was still to be part of Sind, and the British were to govern it on behalf of the amirs. The revenue was to accrue to the British after February 14, 1842, and they were to remit a part of the subsidy equal to one-fifth more than the amount realized from the revenue, which was estimated by the amirs to be Rs. 200,000 and by Captain Postans, who had surveyed the financial possibilities of the areas, as Rs. 117,000 annually. The British were to deduct two lakhs as tribute and give any excess to the amirs. Neither party was to coin money without the other's permission and the treaty was to be concluded between the two parties when a figure acceptable to both was determined as to the annual revenue of Shikarpur.[85]

Outram thought that although the principal amirs of Hyderabad were willing to cede Shikarpur to the British, Mir Shahdad, the third shareholder, also ought to be consulted. He felt that Nasir should be allowed to retain the nominal sovereignty of the place and the amirs should be allowed to coin money, although this last concession was actually of no significance because the Company rupee would soon drive the Hyderabad rupee out of circulation. Outram did not consider that one-fifth of the value of the Shikarpur revenue demanded by the amirs as a bonus was excessive. After all, they had been promised a great fair at Shikarpur as an inducement for their relinquishment of the river tolls, and now they were to lose not only this but to be burdened with the excess civil servants from the area as well.[86]

Calcutta replied to Outram that the Governor-General was willing to accept a perpetual lease of the Hyderabad share of Shikarpur. The British Government would remit to the amirs annually one-fifth more than the average net income derived by the amirs from Shikarpur during the last five or ten years or any other period for which Outram had the means of striking an average. But the amount due for the subsidy payment would of course be subtracted first. Nasir Khan was to be allowed to remain the nominal ruler of the area, although he must recognize that his was only a "divided right of sovereignty." He was to be permitted to maintain a mint but not to operate it.[87]

The only thing, then, that was standing in the way of the cession of the Hyderabad part of Shikarpur to the British was the determination of the number of years to be used in deducing the average revenue. Nasir Khan wanted to use only the past season, which had been a very favorable one, while Outram wished to calculate the average of the last five years or so. A compromise was finally decided on under which the past season

THE AFGHAN CRISIS

was to be used in conjunction with one or two of the preceding years. The transfer was to take place on February 14, 1842, as originally suggested by the amirs, and the final treaty was to be signed once the value of the Shikarpur revenues had been determined to the satisfaction of all.[88]

But despite the apparently successful conclusion of the transaction the negotiations took an abrupt turn when Lieutenant Leckie, having noted the exactions of Suffur Hubshee, the agent of Nasir Khan in Shikarpur, passed on to the amir a letter from Outram to himself which read:

You will point out to his Highness the unjustifiable proceedings of his agent, which, if they excite disturbances in the city, will infallibly render Meer Nusseer Khan personally and individually responsible for whatever losses should be sustained by the inhabitants therefrom; you will immediately call upon his Highness to send immediate orders to his officers at Shikarpore to abstain from any undue exactions, or other proceedings calculated to cause disturbances.[89]

Nasir Khan was furious. He pointed out, with some justice, that what Leckie asked was in direct violation of the second article of the treaty of 1832.[90] He said, "Shikarpore is mine until Major Outram and myself exchange treaties for its transfer." [91] The anticipated transfer never took place, despite a final attempt by Outram in November, 1841, when he wrote to Fort William that Nasir Khan of Khairpur and his brother, Mubarak's heirs, still refused to pay the seven lakhs to Shuja, insisting that they were exempt through the immunity Burnes had granted their father. As a consequence, Outram suggested the seizure of their land in the Shikarpur area.[92] But the Governor-General would not sanction this action, although he told Outram to remind the two amirs that the British could not guarantee them in their possessions until they had paid their share of the tribute.[93]

The pressure of events in Afghanistan soon forced both

questions, at least temporarily, into abeyance, for it became painfully obvious that Shuja, who had regained his throne easily enough, was entirely dependent on the support of British bayonets in order to maintain his position. His return to Kabul with foreign help had served to alienate virtually the whole population, and the departure of British forces would no doubt have resulted in Shah Shuja's immediate overthrow. As the soldiers' presence was a ruinous drain on the exchequer, a disastrous compromise was finally adopted. It was decided to leave the troops quartered in Afghanistan but to curtail drastically the subsidies paid to the Afghan chiefs. Widespread rebellion was the result, and the passes were closed by the aroused tribes.

The details of the ensuing disaster are too well known to bear repetition. Suffice it to say that of the 16,000 men who attempted to extricate themselves from Kabul, only one survived, and that during the crisis both William Macnaghten, the initiator of the Afghan strategy, and Alexander Burnes, whose opinions had so greatly influenced the determination of policy toward Sind, were killed. As for Sind itself, British preponderance was confirmed when the resident was able to replace the family of Syed Soliman Shah as the chief influence in the councils of the amirs,[94] but Sind's future role in the fortunes of the British Empire in India was to be determined by the policy which the Government finally decided to adopt toward Afghanistan and the whole area west of the Indus.

5. Ellenborough, Napier,

and the Amirs of Sind

(1841–1843)

THE AFGHAN REVOLT, which British ineptitude and miscalculation compounded into a major disaster, coincided with the replacement of Auckland as Governor-General by Lord Ellenborough. It is a frequent misconception that Auckland entered the Afghan adventure against the wishes of the home authorities and was recalled because of its failure. Neither of these contentions is true. Not only had Palmerston and Hobhouse recommended and approved the Afghan policy, but the Company and the Board asked Auckland to serve a second term as Governor-General because of their great faith in him. Auckland had already resigned his post, and Ellenborough had been appointed his successor, when the troubles at Kabul commenced.[1]

Upon assuming office in February, 1842, Ellenborough was still dedicated to the same principles that had motivated his policies as President of the Board of Control. He declared British India a satiated state:

Content with the limits nature appears to have assigned to its Empire, the Government of India will devote all of its efforts to the establishment and maintenance of general peace, to the protection of the sovereigns and chiefs, its allies, and to the prosperity and happiness of its own faithful subjects.[2]

He instructed the political agents at native courts to "manifest the utmost personal consideration for the several native princes" to whom they were deputed and to "distinctly understand that the further extension of its dominions forms no part of the policy of the British Government." [3] In a foreign-policy memorandum the Governor-General stated that he considered further expansion would be ill-advised, as it would endanger the stability and welfare of the state and place an excessive strain on its finances.[4] The Secret Committee expressed its "entire and most cordial approbation." [5] But within three years, Lord Ellenborough was to speak of a British India stretching to the "chain of mountains beyond the Indus and the Himalayas as our *ultimate* boundary." [6] He had annexed Sind and had been recalled by the East India Company. The reasons for this reversal of orientation are not hard to assess.

Lord Ellenborough and Sir Charles Napier, the newly appointed commander of British troops in Sind, were in many ways alike—a fact which might have contributed to the great trust Ellenborough placed in the latter. The association, however, of two officials with such similar weaknesses was to influence decisively the future of the amirs of Sind. Both men were highly unpopular. Ellenborough, known by his contemporaries as the "Elephant," [7] was one of the most disliked men of his day; while Napier had never succeeded in willingly obeying any of his superiors. Both were frustrated in their ambitions. Ellenborough was foiled in his attempt to make the Board of Control the stepping stone to the Foreign Office, his real goal.[8] The megalomaniacal Napier, after achieving some distinction in the Peninsular Campaign, spent the next forty years of his life in the obscurity of petty commands and half pay, and received his appointment to India only through the political influence of his brother William. Both considered themselves liberal humanitarians and were romantic in nature. Ellenborough had dreamed of leading an expedition to conquer Egypt;[9] Napier fancied himself as the ruler of all Asia.[10]

Charles Napier, of bizarre appearance, with a vast beard and matted hair, was a man of contradictions: he was capable of great generosity and small-minded parsimony, of humility and unbounded conceit. His military orders reflected both humor and justice.[11] Worshipped by his men,[12] he was often despised by his peers. Napier was the scion of a large and noble house— the great-great-grandson of Charles II through his liaison with Louise de Keroualle. Napier's mother was the fascinating and beautiful Lady Sarah Lennox who twice refused to marry George III, his cousin was Charles James Fox, and his uncle the Duke of Richmond. Charles grew up a proud and head-strong boy full of dreams of military glory. Due to the influence of a relative, General Fox, he received his commission and fought bravely and well in the Corunna campaign, holding temporary command of the 50th Regiment, a responsibility he discharged with considerable skill at a difficult time. Napier was badly wounded and captured in the days following Sir John Moore's death, but after his release and the end of the war he was promoted to lieutenant colonel and given command of the 102d Regiment, which was sent to Bermuda. His career now followed the byways of military service—a command in the War of 1812, two years at Farnham Military College, inspecting field officer in the Ionian Islands—but no glory, only disappointment and humiliation for a mind obsessed with visions of imperial grandeur and public acclaim. His journals are full of personal comparisons with the great men of history:

15 August, Napoleon's birthday: He too is gone and may be met with hereafter. I am at war with half of India: were it the whole I would not care! I laugh them all to scorn.[13]

To-morrow I shall reach Sehwan where Alexander built his tower, and I shall stand where he stood as indeed I have before, but not on the known spot . . .[14] How easily, were I absolute, I could conquer all these countries.[15]

When Napier landed in India he was sixty. If his ambitions were to be satisfied, time was short. "Charles! Charles Napier!" he wrote in his diary, "take heed of your ambition for military glory; you had scotched that snake, but this high command will, unless you are careful, give it all its vigor again. Get thee behind me Satan!" [16] In a similar vein he later confided to his diary:

My God! how humble I feel when I think! How exalted when I behold! I have worked my way to this great command and am grateful at having it, yet despise myself for being so gratified! . . . I despise my worldliness. Am I not past sixty? A few years must kill me; a few days may! And yet I am so weak as to care for these things! No, I do not. I pray to do what is right and just. . . . Alas! I have not the strength! . . . He who takes command loves it.[17]

It is possible that other more practical considerations played a role in Napier's aspirations. He had never been rich and the care of his daughters had frequently been a severe strain on his finances. Upon being congratulated by a fellow officer on his appointment to India, he had replied:

I am very rational, my wishes are only to barter a *great lack of sovereigns* in *this* country for a *lac* of rupees in that! But I am too old for glory now . . . If a man cannot catch glory when his knees are supple, he had better not try when they grow stiff! All I want is to catch the *rupees* for my girls, and then die like a gentleman. I suppose if I survive six years I shall do this.[18]

Napier was indeed destined to survive, and his arrival in Sind coincided with victory in Afghanistan and a resurgence of interest in the Indus, now that affairs to the northwest of the river were well on the way to being settled. On the whole, Auckland had admitted, the amirs of Upper and Lower Sind had behaved in a remarkably temperate manner during the period of British reverses in Afghanistan,[19] especially as intercourse between the British Government and Sind was governed by the 1838–39 treaties forced on the amirs. Yet Outram reported to the Governor-General that Amir Nasir Khan of Hyderabad had been discovered in "treasonable" correspondence with Divan Sanwanmal, the Sikh governor of Multan. The letter, worded ambiguously, vaguely implied some previous understanding for joint action against the British.[20] Outram also intercepted a letter from Mir Rustam Khan to Maharajah Sher Singh of Lahore which intimated a similarly undeveloped plan.[21] The matter did not rest here, for Nasir Khan of Hyderabad was charged with having written Bibarak Bugti, a semi-independent chief of Upper Sind, asking him for aid against the British;[22] and Fateh Mahomed Ghori, Mir Rustam's chief minister, was accused of helping a state prisoner, Mahomed Sharif, to escape to Baluchistan in order to raise an insurrection. Only the first and last of these charges were considered authentic by all the British officers serving in Sind.

Outram had some doubts regarding the authenticity of the letter from Mir Rustam to Sher Singh, because the information leading to its seizure had been supplied by a source inimical to Rustam. Outram thought the letter to be the work of Fateh Mahomed Ghori. George Clerk, the resident at Lahore, shared the reservations of Outram,[23] but Captain Postans, a Persian scholar, who had seen much of Rustam's correspondence, considered the letter to be genuine. As internal evidence to indicate that the letter from Nasir Khan to Bibarak Bugti was a forgery, H. T. Lambrick contends that Nasir Khan would never have addressed a chief who had maintained his independence from his sovereign, the Khan of Kelat, as "an old and trusted friend of this Sarkar." Besides, Bibarak had not extended hospitality to Syed Mahomed Sharif when the latter arrived in Baluchistan to foment his revolt in June, 1842.[24] Only two of the charges against the amirs were definitely true then, and Lord Ellenborough, preoccupied with affairs in Afghanistan, did "not see any necessity for pressing a negotiation upon [the amirs] precipitatively, and on the contrary would rather desire to leave their minds, for the present in tranquility." [25]

On the other hand, T. H. Maddock, one of the Governor-General's secretaries, wrote:

The Governor-General wishes to be informed, whether the territories under Meer Roostum Khan be in such a position as to make it easy to annex a portion thereof to the dominions of the Khan of Bhawulpore, whose dominions his Lordship is desirous of increasing, in reward for his uniform fidelity, and that of his ancestors.[26]

Outram immediately saw possibilities in the idea. He wrote Ellenborough that the district of Sabzalkot in the extreme northeast of Sind had been seized from Bahawalpur by the first generation of Talpurs, and that it now belonged not to a Khairpur amir but to Nasir Khan of Hyderabad, the amir most guilty of behavior unfriendly to the British. The district was three hundred miles from Hyderabad; it was badly governed, and its transfer to Bahawalpur would punish Nasir Khan and put a welcome end to his pretensions to be *rais*. Outram also suggested a scheme whereby the British could remit the tribute due to the Company in return for the cession of Karachi, Sukkur, Bukkur, and two adjacent islands.[27]

The amirs' troubles were just beginning. On September 25, 1842, Napier arrived at Hyderabad for the first time and was handsomely received. Ominously he noted that "possibly this may be the last independent reception they may give as princes to a British general!" [28] Later from Sukkur he wrote that "these Princes do not appear to be acting loyally" and claimed that the amirs were violating the fifth article of the treaty of 1832 by taxing not only their own subjects but those of Bahawalpur.[29] There was indeed some justice to the charge, but as Nasir Khan of Hyderabad wrote to his deputy at Shikarpur when ordering him not to allow boats from Bahawalpur, Mithankot, Shikarpur, and Sabzalkot to pass:

ELLENBOROUGH, NAPIER, AND THE AMIRS OF SIND

You are well aware that the revenues of Sinde depend chiefly upon the grain crops, and if it be allowed to be imported from all quarters, there will be no fixed price, and prices will be uncommonly low, and from the cheapness of grain there will be a deficit in the revenue.[80]

Napier also came into conflict with the amirs regarding their right to tax Sindian boats on the river and goods landed at Karachi. The amirs had previously agreed to allow all country supplies to the British cantonment to be admitted duty free, but this concession had been exploited by their Hindu subjects to evade ordinary taxation. Nasir Khan therefore ordered his agent at Karachi (for Karachi was still nominally Sind territory) to prohibit the merchants of the town from establishing shops in the British camp and to subject all goods landed outside the cantonment limits to customs duties.[81] He considered that the fifth article of the treaty of 1839, which stated that the British would not extend their jurisdiction to his territories nor listen to or encourage complaints against the amirs, a guarantee of his rights. But Napier thought it impossible to let the wording of one article nullify the spirit of the whole treaty and informed the amirs that they must desist from pursuing what he considered to be onerous practices.

On September 11, Ellenborough, reversing his previous stand, decided to open the question of a new treaty with the amirs of Sind.[82] The justification for this course was the assumption that the amirs were guilty of the various accusations against them.[33] He ordered Outram to place before Napier with "judicial accuracy"[84] a statement of the instances when the amirs had violated the terms of the treaties with the British, for he intended to punish any amir who had "evinced hostile designs" during the Afghan war. But, he added, he "would not proceed on this course without ample and convincing evidence of the guilt of the person accused."[35] The amirs, said Ellenborough, would have to make restitution for any infringements on the

Indus and for any duties levied in the British cantonment at Karachi. He authorized Napier to inform the amirs that he was empowered to use force, if necessary, and that the Governor-General was willing to negotiate a new agreement, under the terms of which all tribute would be relinquished in return for the cession of certain areas.[36]

On October 14, Outram prepared for Napier's use his compilation of complaints against the amirs of Upper and Lower Sind as requested by Ellenborough. He urged that a unified government once more be established in Lower Sind. But he pointed out that the Khairpur amirs had never relinquished their right to tax the commerce of their own subjects on the Indus.[37] Outram once more advised the acquisition of Shikarpur as a defensive bastion and trade center. He suggested that the parts of Shikarpur belonging to the two Nasir khans and to Mir Rustam could justifiably be forfeited for their recent intrigues and that the remaining sharers who were not implicated could be compensated.[38]

Napier, after analyzing Outram's return of complaints, forwarded to Ellenborough his observations on the occupation and future of Sind. He agreed with Outram that a single *rais* for Lower Sind should once more be established. It seemed to him that the British had to decide immediately whether they should continue to occupy the positions in Sind which they had acquired in the Afghan war or should evacuate the country altogether. He thought that if they stayed the amirs would continue to infringe on the treaties, while if the British left, force of circumstances would sooner or later prompt their return. The General wrote:

Is it possible that such a state of things can long continue? A Government hated by its subjects, despotic, hostile alike to the interests of the English, and of its own people; a Government of low intrigue, and above all, so constituted that it must, in a few years, fall to pieces by the vice of its own construction; will such a Government, I ask, not maintain an incessant petty hostility against us? Will it not incessantly commit breaches of treaties —those treaties by which alone, we have any right to remain in this country; and therefore must rigidly uphold? I conceive that such a state of political relations could not last, and the more powerful Government would, at no very distant period, swallow up the weaker. If this reasoning be correct, would it not be better to come to the results at once? [39]

Napier proposed to punish the amirs for the "treasonable" letters and the treaty violations by requiring the cession of Sukkur, Bukkur, Sabzalkot, Karachi, and, for commercial purposes, Shikarpur. In return for this, all tribute would be relinquished and the British agent would be recalled from Hyderabad. In regard to Outram's contention that the amirs of Khairpur were not bound to desist from taxing their subjects, he held that "to excuse the Ameers upon the ground that others are not equally coerced, is answered by coercing the others." [40]

Ellenborough's main concern was still to reward the Khan of Bahawalpur. In hope that the amirs would commit some overt act, the Governor-General wrote to Napier:

If you are under the necessity of making any movement of Troops towards Hyderabad then Meer Nusseer Khan will forfeit all his property and right on Karrachee, Tatta, Shikapoor, Sukkur, the Pergunnahs adjoining Bhawalpore country and Subzulcote and all the property and rights in these last Districts, whatever they may be, shall immediately be transferred to the Khan of Bhawalpore. [41]

But Ellenborough left Napier full descretion to verify the charges on which any new treaty was to be based. He wrote:

You are much more competent to decide on the spot as to the authenticity of the letters attributed to Meer Nusseer and Meer Roostum Khan than I am here, and I am prepared to abide by and support your decision. . . . If a Government were to

ELLENBOROUGH, NAPIER, AND THE AMIRS OF SIND

wait in every case of suspected hostile intentions until it obtained such proof of the hostile intention, as would be sufficient to convict the person suspected in a Court of Justice, it would in most cases expose itself at once to disgrace and disaster— It is necessary to proceed upon a strong presumption of intended hostility where hesitation might seriously affect great national interests.[42]

Despite the evidence to the contrary Napier was convinced "that every letter was really written by the Ameers and that nothing is wanted but an opportunity to attack us." [43]

Ellenborough now decided to dispense with the services of the political officers in Sind, as he felt that these agents exercised power even in military affairs. He dispatched to Napier orders closing down the Sind-Baluchistan political department as of November 15, 1842.[44] This left him entirely dependent on Napier for information, because the politicals who had not come under the jurisdiction of the military were now removed from the scene. The elimination of the agency also cut off Napier's prime and most reliable source of intelligence. After this he was forced to rely on Major T. Clibborn—known to his contemporaries as "Moonshine Clibborn"—whom he made head of his intelligence department. Neither Ellenborough nor Maddock had much knowledge about Sind; Napier knew nothing about Sind nor about India. He had had experience in military and administrative posts, but his current problem was a political one, and for this type of situation he would seem to have been the worst of all possible choices. "Mene! mene! tekel, upharsin!" he wrote in his diary, "How is all this to end? We have no right to seize Scinde, yet we shall do so, and a very advantageous, useful, humane piece of rascality it will be." [45] The situation could have been retrieved only by an astute choice of assistants; but Napier chose Mr. Richardson, a man of no ability or stature whatever, and Lieutenant E. J. Brown, who was not lacking in ability but tended to be abrupt, and

ELLENBOROUGH, NAPIER, AND THE AMIRS OF SIND

whose administration of affairs in Upper Sind was constantly the subject of complaint. He spoke no Persian, Sindhi, or Baluchi.[46] E. B. Eastwick wrote of him: "No man who swallows from one to two dozen bottles of beer per diem can always scrutinize with sufficient exactness the infinitesimal limits of the expedient and the inexpedient." [47]

It was on these men, along with his personal staff consisting of Major Macpherson and his nephew William Napier, that the General had to depend for advice and assistance. Napier, with the discontinuation of the political agency, had *carte blanche* and, due to the slowness of communications, virtually unlimited power to act as he saw fit. Ellenborough wrote to Wellington concerning the validity of the accusations against the amirs: "I have left the matter in Sir C. Napier's hands." [48] Napier himself said:

My design and hope is to find excuses for acting on my own responsibility and going right before there is time to set me wrong! . . . It is yet to be proved how I command a large force or rather a small one in the face of the enemy.[49]

Wellington informed Ellenborough that the Cabinet was dissatisfied with his having left the conduct of affairs in Sind entirely to the discretion of Sir Charles Napier,[50] but the Governor-General was charmed with the General and blind to his obvious defects. "I can assure you," he wrote to Sir George Arthur, the Governor of Bombay, "it is a comfort to me I cannot describe to have a man in whom I can so entirely trust at Sukkur." [51]

The amirs, who were now becoming increasingly disquieted by rumors of the new treaty, feared that the General was about to march on Khairpur, and in terror sent out a call for troops. Napier himself was ever more convinced of the baseness of the Talpurs and did little to assuage their fears. He wrote in his diary, "My mind is . . . made up: if they fire a shot, Scinde shall be annexed to India." [52] Later he informed Ellenborough that the amirs were raising forces for an internal struggle but that

> barbarians become quickly reconciled when a common enemy appears. The Ameers think that General England's force [which was returning from service in Afghanistan] is coming with some evil object against them and they become friends. They imagine that we are going to give Shikarpore to Persia.[53]

Napier could probably have disabused the amirs of these notions if he had only made the attempt, but he failed to do so.

Meanwhile, Ellenborough, on November 2, had received Napier's lengthy comments on the situation in Sind, supplemented by fifty-seven enclosures, and had found one day sufficient to digest the contents. He wrote to the General that Rustam, despite his former friendliness, would have to be punished for his letter to Sher Singh and for Fateh Mahomed Ghori's complicity in the escape of Mahomed Sharif. The heirs of Mubarak would not have to pay back tribute since Mubarak had not entered into a treaty with the Company, but they could not expect British protection. The Governor-General also felt that a policy of exchanging territory for tribute should be encouraged, because the collection of tribute was a constant irritation and placed the British in a bad light, while the mulcting of territory was an injury soon forgotten. To this effect the Governor-General proposed to gain the cession of Karachi, Rohri, Sukkur, Bukkur, and the necessary arrondissements. He advocated the creation of a uniform currency for all India and, as part of this scheme, planned a common coinage for Sind with the head of the British sovereign on one side and a native symbol on the other. The right to cut wood along the banks of the Indus was to be secured despite the fact that coal might turn out to be a more economical fuel for steamers.[54]

The most important of Ellenborough's proposals centered on

his oft-mentioned desire to reward the Khan of Bahawalpur. He intended to give Sabzalkot and Bhung Bhara to the Khan, as well as the land between Sabzalkot and Rohri. He felt that this would provide the British with a continuous line of friendly territory along the left bank of the Sutlej and Indus from Ferozepur to Rohri, thus enabling them to shift the line of communications to the Northwest provinces of India from the Ganges to the Indus and to show the other Indian princes that the British knew how to reward as well as how to punish. It is to be noted that all these areas were the possession of Nasir Khan of Khairpur and not of his namesake Nasir Khan of Hyderabad, who was thought to be guilty of the correspondence with Bibarak Bugti and Divan Sanwanmal. The Governor-General had confused the two in his mind—a mistake which was to cause grave consequences in the future.[55]

Ellenborough had not lost sight of his aspirations for the development of the Indus commerce but he did not include in his dispatches about the proposed new treaty any provision for complete freedom of trade in Sind, because this was considered impractical and impossible to enforce. He did, however, write:

My ultimate object is the entire freedom of internal trade throughout the whole territory between the Hindoo Coosh, the Indus and the sea, and I only await the favorable occasion for effecting this purpose and for introducing uniformity of currency within the same limits. . . . These various measures which would impart to the whole people of India the most desirable of advantages desired from Union under the same Empire, it may require much time to effect.[56]

Ellenborough labored under the same delusions as his predecessors regarding the possibilities for trade on the Indus. In October he asked the Court for six steamers to carry English goods and military stores straight up the Indus to the Northwest, "to save time, lives and money." [57] He felt that in a very short time steamboats belonging to the merchants of Bombay would carry British manufactures to the Northwest. He wrote Napier that as soon as Sukkur was acquired, the General was to build a large *serai*[58] for merchants, combining the beauty of the East and the fortifications of the West. Sukkur, Bukkur, and Rohri were to be fused into a magnificent entrepôt to be called the "City of Victoria on the Indus." [59] But the passage of years had not improved the navigability of the Indus, and once again a Governor-General was to be disappointed in his ambitions to exploit the river.

When the drafts of the new treaties arrived in Sukkur on November 12,[60] they were shown to Outram, who was about to leave. In his *Commentary* Outram stated that he had pointed out to Napier that the demand for vast amounts of territory from the amirs of Upper Sind must be a mistake.[61] Had he seen Ellenborough's dispatch, which accompanied the draft treaties, his suspicions would have been confirmed, for Ellenborough again clearly indicated that he had confused Nasir Khan of Hyderabad with his kinsman, Nasir Khan of Khairpur.[62] There is no evidence that Napier ever advised Ellenborough of the mistake, nor did he rectify it himself although the Governor-General's instructions empowered him to do so.

The Amirs of course balked at the exactions of the proposed treaties and claimed they were innocent of the charges leveled against them. Intelligence reports showed that they were greatly alarmed at the removal of the agency from Sind and Baluchistan, and especially at the departure of Major Outram. The amirs feared they were to be left at the mercy of the Afghan tribes.[63] Further dispatches reported that the amirs had ordered the Jam of the Jokhias and the Chandio Sardar, both chiefs of tribes west of the Indus, to be prepared to defend their frontiers, and that Mir Rustam had sent a message to the Lower Sind amirs taunting them for their "supineness in not collecting troops, when so large a body of men is assembled at Sukkur, to oppose which the Upper Scinde Ameers are prepared." [64]

ELLENBOROUGH, NAPIER, AND THE AMIRS OF SIND

Reports of warlike preparations by the amirs continued to pour in to Napier's headquarters from Major Clibborn's intelligence department, but Rustam indicated his peaceful intentions by arranging through his minister, Fateh Mahomed Ghori, to meet Napier at Sukkur on November 14. At the last moment the old man was persuaded by his relatives that the meeting with Napier would only result in his betrayal, and he tried to change the meeting place to Abad, four miles down the river from Rohri.[65] This Napier would not accept, and the meeting never took place. Clibborn meanwhile reported that Nasir Khan of Hyderabad had informed Rustam of his intention of sending his son and his nephew to Khairpur with a force of 16,000 men to oppose the British.[66] Clibborn, in intelligence covering November 15 to 20, reported hostile maneuvers by the amirs, particularly in Upper Sind, but a group of Baluchi horsemen sent to observe the Larkhana district found little out of the ordinary.[67]

Where Mir Rustam failed in gaining an interview with Napier, his younger brother Mir Ali Murad succeeded. He had been sent by the Khairpur Talpurs chiefly as a family emissary, but his conversation with the General concentrated on the future of the Turban—the hereditary chieftainship of the amirs of Upper Sind. Napier wrote to Ellenborough: "I this day had a meeting with Meer Ali Moorad. His object was to know if we could secure him the Turban of Chieftaincy." Napier agreed to support Ali Murad's claim to the Turban at Rustam's death, and the former's claim to the chieftainship was indeed valid, because the title descended from brother to brother rather than from father to son. Napier explained his proposed course of action to the Governor-General:

1. It is just. Ali Moorad has the right to the 'turban' for his own life, after the death of Meer Roostum, and it promises to protect him in his right.
2. It detaches Ali Moorad from any league among the Ameers and consequently diminishes the chances of bloodshed.

82

ELLENBOROUGH, NAPIER, AND THE AMIRS OF SIND

3. It lays a train to arrive at a point which I think should be urged viz., that we should treat with *one* Ameer, instead of a number. This will simplify our Political dealings with these Princes, and gradually reduce them to the class of rich noblemen, and their chief will be perfectly dependent on the Government of India; living as he will do close to this large station [Sukkur].[68]

In contrast, the General, whose virtues did not include consistency, wrote in his journal of the same day:

Who gets this puggree turban is to me moonshine as they really have no fixed rule. . . . But my strong suspicion is that Roostam will force me to deprive himself of the Turban, and of his kingdom too! [69]

Lambrick thinks that Napier gave a hint of these views in his conversation with Ali Murad and thus set the stage for future machinations concerning the Turban.[70]

From this moment the incidence of reports on the warlike preparations of the amirs increased. Whether Ali Murad acted as *agent provocateur* is hard to determine. But certainly Napier's brusque manner and precipitate actions did not help matters. When one of Rustam's agents taxed a Bahawalpur merchant in violation of the treaty, Napier informed the old chief:

I shall determine unless your Highness doth immediately comply with these demands [to desist] . . . that these various and insulting violations of the Treaty have been committed with your sanction and I shall treat you as an Enemy.[71]

Falsely claiming that he was acting on the specific orders of the Governor-General, Napier issued Rustam an ultimatum:

I have ordered six regiments to be ready to move at a moment's notice with which I shall cross the river and march upon Khyrpoor if my messenger returns either insulted or with a refusal to comply with the conditions proposed. I have desired him to wait but *two hours* for his answer.[72]

The Governor-General expressed his approval of Napier's action and, needless to say, Rustam hastened to comply with the General's request. Ellenborough hoped that the presence of six regiments would obviate bloodshed, "but I very much fear that until our force has been actually felt, there will be no permanent observance of the existing Treaty or of any new Treaty we may make." [73]

It was now decided to recall Outram to be the commissioner for the negotiation of the new treaties with the amirs. It would of course take him some time to return to Sind, and Napier, in no mood to wait, wrote, "I had no intention of waiting for Major Outram's arrival. . . . I mean to consult no one; I see my way clearly." He conjectured that there were three months of cool weather before him, long enough, he thought, to decide any quarrel with the amirs, before the hot weather.[74]

Napier arranged that the draft treaties would reach the amirs of Khairpur and Hyderabad simultaneously. There is no evidence that he ever explained to the amirs of Upper Sind, who were innocent of treachery, that they would be compensated for any loss of territory claimed under the new treaty, nor was Nasir Khan of Khairpur informed as to why he was mulcted so heavily. None of the Governor-General's letters which accompanied the treaties mentioned any culpable conduct attributable to this chief. Even the letter intended for him was sent by Napier to Nasir Khan of Hyderabad who was indeed the amir accused of the "treasonable" conduct but who was left relatively free of territorial loss by the treaty. The only reference to Mir Nasir Khan of Khairpur at all was a passing remark in the letter to Mir Rustam. Nevertheless, the Khairpur *vakils* sent to confer with Napier reported to their masters that the General appeared friendly and generously disposed toward them, and they consequently offered Napier the amirs' submission. Rustam as a result discharged many of the levies he had in desperation recruited.[75] But Napier informed Ellenborough that he thought the Khairpur amirs were only playing for time in order to make common cause with their cousins of Hyderabad.

On December 8 Napier issued a proclamation announcing that no land taxes were in future to be paid to the amirs in the areas to be ceded under the provisions of the proposed new treaty, and later in the month Colonel Wallace led the regiments of the Bengal army out of Rohri into these districts.[76] This action, taken on Napier's initiative, resulted in the Khairpur amirs' hastily trying to recall some of their discharged troops, as they were alarmed at the implementation of an article of a treaty which had not yet even been signed.[77] When unfounded rumors reached Napier that the amirs of Khairpur were contemplating a night attack on his camp, he wrote Rustam:

Your submission to the order of the Governor-General and your friendship for our nation should be beyond doubt. . . . We are friends. . . . It is therefore right to inform you of strange rumours that reach me. Your subjects (it is said) propose to attack my camp in the night time. This would of course be very foolish, because my soldiers would slay those who attacked them, and when day dawned, I would march to Khyrpore and destroy your capital city, with the exception of your Highnesses [sic] palace which I would leave standing alone as a mark of respect for Your Highness.[78]

Napier added that he would then reimburse himself from the Khairpur treasury.

Lieutenant Stanley, who had carried the draft treaties to the amirs of Hyderabad, reported that they would not resist the General nor the conclusion of the treaty,[79] but Napier preferred to believe the inaccurate reports of local spies that the 10,000 Baluchis gathered at Larkhana were preparing to attack Shikarpur.[80] He felt Clibborn's highly colored reports only confirmed his theory that all the amirs except Sobdar of Hyderabad

ELLENBOROUGH, NAPIER, AND THE AMIRS OF SIND

and Ali Murad of Khairpur were bent on war. On December 12 he wrote to Rustam:

I laugh at your preparations for war. . . . Eight days have now passed, and I have not heard that your Highness has nominated a commissioner of rank to arrange the details of the Treaty. . . . Your Highness is collecting troops in all directions, I must therefore have your acceptance of the Treaty immediately—yea or nay.[81]

Rustam replied:

God knows, we have no intention of opposing the British, nor a thought of war or fighting. We have not the power. . . . If, without any fault on my part, you choose to seize my territory by force, I shall not oppose you, but I shall consent to and observe the provisions of the new Treaty.[82]

The Hyderabad emissaries deputed to conclude the treaty with the General arrived at Sukkur on December 15, and Napier received them the following day. The agents of Sobdar and Hussein Ali Khan were particularly ready with professions of loyalty and friendship for the British, while those of Mir Mir Mahomed and Nasir Khan spoke of the value and importance they attributed to the British connection.[83]

This promising course of events came to an abrupt halt on the night of December 17 when the mails were looted between Khairpur and Rohri. Napier blamed Rustam and wrote him:

My letters have been stopped near Khyrpore; that has been done either by your order or without your consent. If by your order, you are guilty; if without your consent, you can not command your people. In either case, I order you to disband your armed followers instantly. I will go to Khyrpore to see that this order is obeyed.[84]

ELLENBOROUGH, NAPIER, AND THE AMIRS OF SIND

Rustam explained that he had no knowledge of the mail robbery and indeed would have made an effort to protect mail shipments if he had ever been warned to do so. He suggested that the General send an officer to Khairpur to report to him on happenings in that place and again protested his loyalty and friendship for the Birtish.[85]

Napier received Rustam's letter on the night of December 18. Lambrick points out that it was accepted by a certain *munshi*, Mohiuddin, who later that evening informed Lieutenant Brown of a verbal communication delivered by the chief's messenger, expressing Rustam's desire of fleeing to Napier's camp. Despite the fact that Mohiuddin had three times been reported to have taken bribes for rendering various services to the amirs,[86] Napier accepted this information without personally interviewing Mohiuddin or Rustam's messenger.[87]

This latest turn of events prompted the General to advocate the replacement of the senile old prince with his young pro-British brother, Ali Murad, if not as *rais*, at least as the actual determiner of policy. Consequently he wrote to Rustam:

My own belief is, that, personally you have ever been the friend of the English. But you are helpless among your ill-judging family. I send this by your brother, his Highness Ali Moorad; listen to his advice; trust yourself to his care. . . . Follow my advice, it is that of a friend.[88]

To Ellenborough he wrote:

I had a secret message from Meer Roostum . . . that Roostum could do nothing, and would escape to my camp. I did not like this, as it would have embarrassed me very much how to act; but the idea struck me at once that he might go to Ali Moorad who might induce him (as a family arrangement) to resign the Turban to him (Ali Moorad), . . . I therefore secretly wrote to Roostum and Ali Moorad, and about one o'clock this morning I had an express from Ali Moorad, to say that his brother is safe

ELLENBOROUGH, NAPIER, AND THE AMIRS OF SIND

with him. . . . Ali Moorad is now virtually chief; for if Meer Roostum does not bestow the Turban upon him, he will at all events, be guided by Ali, in whose hands he has voluntarily thrown himself. . . . The chief of the Talpoors, frightened at the violence of his family, and our steady operations to coerce them, has thrown himself into his brother's power at my advice, otherwise I should believe some trick was intended.[89]

On the 21st Napier received the expected letter from Rustam stating that he had abdicated the Turban in favor of Ali Murad "according to the wishes of the illustrious English government." [90] It is not surprising that Rustam thought he was acting on Napier's direct command as the General's "advice" was quite probably unsolicited. Napier's chief interest was that Ali Murad be the *de facto* ruling chief in Upper Sind; whether he was actually *rais* did not seem of too much importance. In view of a possible hostile reaction, Napier, on the 23d, wrote to Ali Murad:

I think your Highness will do well not to assume the Turban for the following reasons. People will say that the English put it on your head against the will of Meer Roostum. But do as you please. I only give you my advice as a friend who wishes to see you great and powerful in Scinde. This is the wish of my Government. The Governor-General has approved of all I have said to you.[91]

He explained his actions to Ellenborough on the 27th:

This [the desirability of replacing Mir Rustam as *rais* in Upper Sind with Ali Murad] made me venture to promise Ali Moorad your Lordship's support in having the Turban, which your Lordship has approved of. The next step was to secure him the exercise of its power now, even during his brother's life. This I was so fortunate to succeed in, by persuading Meer Roostum to place himself in Ali Murad's hands.[92]

ELLENBOROUGH, NAPIER, AND THE AMIRS OF SIND

On December 23 the envoys of Mir Shahdad Khan of Hyderabad met Napier and indicated their chief's acceptance of the new treaty. Thus, as Lambrick indicates, Napier was able to report that all the amirs of Upper and Lower Sind had accepted the provisions of the treaty within three weeks of their presentation. But matters were yet far from settled. On the 21st Rustam's sons and nephews had fled from Khairpur, leaving the city to Ali Murad, and on the 28th Rustam himself escaped from his brother's fort at Kot Diji. The next day he wrote to the General that he had been forced to abdicate by Ali Murad. Napier reacted by issuing on January 1 a proclamation to the people of Sind advising them of the abdication of Rustam and the circumstances surrounding the acquisition of the Turban by Ali Murad. He said: "I will, according to the existing Treaty, protect the chief, Ameer Ali Moorad, in his rights, as justly constituted chieftain of the Talpoor family." [93]

The next day he wrote to Rustam himself:

You make a submission to me as the representative of his Excellency the Governor-General; you have solemnly resigned the Turban, and you now avow that you look upon this —the most solemn act of your life, as a farce and a mockery! Ameer, I do not understand such double conduct. I hold you to your words and deeds: I no longer consider you to be the chief of the Talpoors, nor will I treat with you as such, nor with those who consider you to be Rais.[94]

6. The Annexation and Its Repercussions
(1843–1850)

DESPITE THE ACCEPTANCE of the treaty by the amirs, the march toward hostilities was not halted, because the forced transfer of the Turban from Rustam to Ali Murad and Napier's declared intention of instituting the rule of primogeniture in the succession—a violation of time-honored custom and tradition—roused the Baluchis to action, where the deprivation of lands and revenues had not.

Intelligence from Clibborn soon informed Napier that the Upper Sind amirs had moved with what forces they had in the direction of Hyderabad,[1] but Napier decided that a more likely retreat was Imamgarh, a desert fortress belonging to Mir Mahomed Khan, a nephew of Rustam's. He wrote Ellenborough:

The Ameers put implicit faith in their deserts, and feel confident that we can not reach them. . . . I made up my mind that, although war had not been declared (nor is it necessary to declare it), I would at once march upon Emaum Ghur, and prove to the whole Talpoor family of both Khyrpore and Hyderabad, that neither their deserts, nor their negotiations, can protect them from the British Troops.[2]

Clibborn's reports for the end of December and early January pointed to the collection of a force of more than 5,000 men under the leadership of some of Rustam's disgruntled relatives at Dhinji, sixty miles to the south of Khairpur, while 2,000

90

ANNEXATION AND ITS REPERCUSSIONS

more were supposedly with Mir Rustam. Mir Ali Akbar, Rustam's second son, was said to be raising a force at Shahgarh, a fort about one hundred miles in the desert east of Khairpur. Yet the intelligence made it clear that these preparations were directed against Ali Murad and not against the British.[3] A Hindu spy sent to Dhinji gauged the force there at only 600-700 men,[4] and on January 5, Clibborn's Baluchi and Khyeri cavalry returned with an estimate of a maximum of 2,500 men and four guns.[5]

Since the forces of the principal Khairpur fugitives were so small, Napier could proceed with his plans against Imamgarh. On the first night of the march the force stopped at Nara, only a short distance from Mir Rustam's encampment, and the General sent the newly arrived Outram to visit the chief. He told Outram,

I only agreed to his (the Ameer's) being made easy as to his personal safety; but that no concession or submission could reinstate him in the Turban, which he had resigned and upon which I consider the tranquillity of Sinde to depend.[6]

Outram took with him Lieutenant Brown and Sheik Ali Hussein (Ali Murad's minister) to assuage any possible suspicions the latter might have. The aged chief, encamped in miserable conditions, denied to Outram that he had ever sent the secret message to Napier on which future transactions concerning the Turban rested so heavily. He said that he had abdicated under pressure from Ali Murad, who among other things had promised to look after the interest of the Khairpur Talpurs through his influence with the General. He had been warned that Napier still intended to make him a prisoner and hence had escaped from Diji.[7] Rustam wanted to see the General in person, but he looked so ill that Outram prevailed on him to send his son Ali Akbar and one of his nephews. The two deputies duly saw Napier, who informed them that Rustam could keep his own

ANNEXATION AND ITS REPERCUSSIONS

lands but not those he held as *Rais*. When the young amirs left, Napier shook hands with them as a token of friendship. Lambrick suggests that Rustam's agents paid a courtesy visit to their uncle, Ali Murad, before they left the British camp and that he convinced them that they should abandon Rustam's cause and join him in order to gain the security of their possessions. A spy of Outram's in Rustam's camp reported that the two envoys totally misrepresented Napier's message and only emphasized his hostility toward Rustam.[8]

Meanwhile, Napier decided to blow up Imamgarh in spite of having written Ellenborough that he would send word to the amirs "that I am not going to plunder or slay them, if they do not make resistance." [9] On January 11, Imamgarh was obliterated, and Napier wrote in his journal:

The light was grand and hellish beyond description; the volume of smoke, fire and embers flying up was a throne fit for the devil! I do not like this work of destruction, but reason tells me two things. First it will prevent bloodshed, and it is better to destroy temples made by men than temples built by the Almighty. Second, this castle was built and used for oppression, and in future its ruins will shelter the slave instead of the tyrant.[10]

He informed Ellenborough that the fort was full of gunpowder and grain,[11] when actually the 10,000 pounds of powder found were old and caked and the supply of grain was small.[12] It is worthwhile to mention, after Napier's flight of rhetoric, that the fort was deserted, with no troops in occupation.

Rustam now again petitioned Napier for reinstatement, but to no avail, and with the destruction of Imamgarh added to Rustam's crown of thorns Rustam was not to be consoled. He wrote: "What remains to be settled? Our means of livelihood are taken. Why am I not to continue as Rais for the short time I have left to live?" [13] Napier sent Outram with a conciliatory message to the hold man, and then ordered the commissioner

92

ANNEXATION AND ITS REPERCUSSIONS

to proceed to Khairpur to meet on January 20 with the envoys of all the amirs of Upper and Lower Sind to settle the terms of the treaty, as the deadline for its conclusion was January 25. To the amirs he wrote:

If any Vakeel [envoy] shall declare that he has not [full] . . . powers, I will exclude him from the meeting and consider that his master refuses to treat; and I will enter the territories of such Ameer with the troops under my orders, and take possession of them in the name of the British Government.[14]

Outram, upon his arrival at Khairpur, was to adjust the details of the new treaty; however, his power was greatly circumscribed in that he could not change the disposition of land prescribed by the treaty nor alter any of the recent enactments and arrangements concerning the Turban. He did, however, suggest to Napier that the provision of the treaty placing the Queen's head on one side of Sindian coins was objectionable as contrary to Moslem custom and should be deleted from the proposed agreement.[15] More urgently he strongly advised Napier to send Brown to accompany Rustam to Khairpur, for he feared that otherwise Ali Murad, whom Outram suspected of having illegally deprived Rustam of the Turban, would prevent the former *rais* from appearing on the appointed day. Rustam's failure to sign the treaty would enhance British hostility toward him, and his absence would of course prevent him from telling his version of the Turban episode.[16] But Napier chose to ignore this advice, although he did promise to pass on to Ellenborough Outram's opinion that it was inadvisable to deprive the friendly Mir Hussein Ali of Tatta.[17]

On January 22 Outram reported to Napier that all envoys from Lower Sind were in Khairpur, but not those of Upper Sind:

I am positively sick, and doubtless you are tired, of these petty intrigues, brother against brother, and son against father—and

93

ANNEXATION AND ITS REPERCUSSIONS

sorry that we should be in any way the instruments to be worked upon by such blackguards; for, in whatever way we act, we must play into the hands of one party or the other, unless we take the whole country to ourselves.[18]

Outram had always felt that Ali Murad was the greatest rascal and charlatan of the whole Talpur family, and since Rustam had indeed failed to appear in Khairpur Outram took this as proof that Ali Murad had succeeded in his design of preventing Rustam's attendance at the meeting. Outram suggested that even if the Upper Sind emissaries did not appear, the treaty should be promulgated [19] and that he should be allowed to proceed to Hyderabad to save the amirs of Lower Sind from foolishness similar to that of their cousins of Khairpur.[20] Napier agreed with Outram about promulgating the treaty, if necessary, without the consent of all the amirs but he reacted strongly against Outram's other suggestions. He wrote:

It will be impossible for you to leave Khyrpur; *we must open* our treaty on the *25th*, or we should give first cause of complaint. . . . Besides Roostam has a right to go where he likes, and I have more to take offense? My letter gives him his choice of attending personally, or sending his Vakeel, which he perhaps will do; I therefore propose to halt till I hear what passes on the 25th, and then act as circumstances dictate.[21]

On January 24 Outram reiterated his request to be allowed to go to Hyderabad because he had with him at Khairpur only Ali Murad's minister—none of the other Upper Sind amirs having appeared or sent representatives—and the envoys of the Hyderabad amirs, who, with the exception of the emissaries of Mirs Sobdar and Hussein Ali, were not fully empowered, since they had apparently left the capital before Napier's circular had arrived. Outram argued:

Whatever remains to be settled between us and the chiefs of Hyderabad can be more speedily and satisfactorily arranged with

ANNEXATION AND ITS REPERCUSSIONS

them at their own capital. . . . By going to Hyderabad I should afford one more chance to the fugitive Ameers, for doubtless the Ameers of Hyderabad will intercede for them. . . . I should prevent those [Hyderabad] chiefs also bolting, and so adding to our embarrassments.[22]

Outram added that he doubted that the Khairpur amirs would willingly accede to the terms of the treaty in view of the extensive redistribution of the revenues of Upper Sind. Under existing conditions the income of all the Upper Sind amirs was Rs. 2,039,500, of which Ali Murad's share was Rs. 295,500. Now, because of the new treaty, the amirs were losing Rs. 610,500 per annum due to the territory ceded to Bahawalpur, leaving a total of Rs. 1,429,000, of which Ali Murad was to receive Rs. 445,000.[23] In addition, Ali Murad was to acquire one-fourth of the remaining property of Sind, or Rs. 357,250, which accrued to the *rais* for the support of the chieftainship under a rule initiated by Mir Sohrab, the founder of the Khairpur dynasty. When Mir Sohrab ruled, there were only four chiefs to share the total income and the *rais* was responsible for the defense of the realm. Now there were eighteen chiefs with separate establishments, and the British had assumed the duties of protection. Under the new arrangement Ali Murad, who had only three sons, controlled a revenue of Rs. 802,250 annually; while all that remained for the support of the other amirs, their feudal chiefs and dependents, as well as most of the Baluch *sirdars* who had hitherto held *jagirs* in the territory to be made over to Ali Murad under the provisions of the Treaty of Nunahar, was Rs. 625,750 in place of the Rs. 1,744,000 they had formerly enjoyed.[24]

What Outram had to say made good sense, but Napier was in no mood to listen. On January 27 he addressed a proclamation to the amirs of Upper Sind giving them until February 1 to send envoys to his headquarters. They would be treated as

ANNEXATION AND ITS REPERCUSSIONS

friends until this date, but any mir who did not comply by the deadline would be treated as an enemy:

Ameers, you imagine that you can procrastinate till your fierce sun drives the British troops out of the field, and forces them to seek shelter in Sukkur. You trusted to your desert and were deceived; you trust to your deadly sun and may again be deceived. I will not write a second letter to you, nor a second time expose the authority which I represent to indignity, but this proclamation will, I hope, induce you to adopt a manly instead of an insidious attitude.[25]

Napier did report to Ellenborough that the Khairpur opposition to the treaty was based on the loss of territory to Bahawalpur which they felt would bankrupt them,[26] but he neglected to discuss the dissatisfaction engendered by Ali Murad's accession to the Turban. To Outram he wrote:

If we are unjust in being here at all, at least let the people and ourselves draw from that injustice the benefit of civilization. This is my view, and I really think the Ameers' interests form a very minute ingredient in the business: least of all Roostam, who seems to have no good or manly qualification. Why then support Ali Murad? . . . because a man with three ideas is better than one who has none.[27]

Outram's response was direct and forceful. He thought it unwise to overthrow the patriarchal form of government which had so long persisted in Sind:

It grieves me to say that my heart, and the judgment God has given me, unite in condemning the measures we are carrying out for his Lordship as most tyrannical—positive robbery. I consider, therefore, that every life which may hereafter be lost in consequence will be a murder.[28]

96

ANNEXATION AND ITS REPERCUSSIONS

He felt that the recent troubles in Sind were the fault of the British, who had abolished the *rais* in Lower Sind and subverted its counterpart in Khairpur. The elevation of Ali Murad threatened the very policy the British were attempting to establish as Ali Murad was opposed by all his relatives, and his foreign mercenaries would dispossess many of the Baluch *sirdars*, thus fomenting the very unrest the British were trying to avoid along the Indus. The only alternative to the *status quo* was British annexation of the whole area, which would necessitate its occupation by numerous garrisons. Outram questioned "whether we should by that means either pay our expenses, benefit the people, or preserve tranquility, leaving alone the unwarrantable outrage against justice and good faith we should commit." [29] Sir George Arthur, the Governor of Bombay, had foretold the rise of differences between Napier and Outram:

For although I entertain a very high opinion of Major Outram's talents both as a soldier and a politician, yet I suspect he has a temper of his own, and will not very cheerfully brook the interference of a military superior. Whilst on the other hand, General Napier, though by no means difficult to manage has I apprehend the organ of firmness more strongly developed than that of amenity. [30]

Outram belonged to that small group of high-minded and self-less British civil servants who from time to time appeared on the imperial stage. He had served with distinction in the Afghan war and was destined to be immortalized by his exploits during the Mutiny. His life was devoted not only to the service of the Queen but also to the welfare (at least as he saw it) of the people he governed on her behalf or to whom he was deputed as a representative of the Government of India. Napier had never pretended to like people who disagreed with him. At one time he had held a high opinion of Outram, and at a dinner following the dissolution of the Sind-Baluchistan Political Department had even offered the toast which was to remain linked forever with Outram's name: "Gentlemen, I give you the 'Bayard of India,' *sans peur et sans reproche,* Major James Outram, of the Bombay Army." [31] Now relations between the two deteriorated rapidly and culminated in the war of polemics which the General and his erstwhile subordinate were to wage for many years after the annexation of Sind. "My worst sin," Napier later wrote, "is to wish to shoot Outram as he deserves, for he is base to the last degree." [32]

But the final break was still some months off, and on January 28, Napier wrote to Outram permitting him to go to Hyderabad.[33] The letter never reached the commissioner, and he remained chafing at the bit in Khairpur. On the same day John Jacob, the commander of the Scinde Irregular Horse, was sent with a detachment of 500 men to reconnoiter the Khairpur amirs' position at Kunhera, less than fifty miles from Hyderabad. He reported that the camp contained no more than 1,300 to 1,400 people, including armed followers, women, and camp followers. This number was slightly augmented when Rustam joined the encampment with his family from Nara.[34]

As Napier marched and countermarched through Sind, the amirs became increasingly alarmed; but on January 30 three emissaries representing Mirs Nasir Khan, Mahomed, and Shahdad, fully empowered to sign the treaty, saw Napier approaching with his whole army. They had come in response to the General's letter of January 15 and he, as Lambrick indicates, by forcing them to sign the treaty at that moment, could have settled the matter once and for all, at least as far as the Hyderabad amirs were concerned—especialy as Outram had already gained the compliance of the agents of Sobdar and Hussein Ali.[35] This Napier failed to do. But he warned the *vakils* that unless he had heard by the fifth of the next month that they had convinced the Upper Sind Talpurs to meet Outram at Hyderabad he would consider them his enemies. Napier bound himself to remain at Bhiria until that date but he did not convince the Hyderabad

ANNEXATION AND ITS REPERCUSSIONS

emissaries of his pacific intentions, for Mirza Khusru Beg, the leader of the delegation, reported to his master, "The General is bent upon war, so get ready." [36]

Outram meanwhile waited restlessly in Khairpur for word from Napier, and when none was forthcoming by February 1 he left without orders, assuming correctly that Napier's letter had somehow gone astray.[37] Napier, for his part, not having heard of Rustam's arrival in Hyderabad by February 5, recommenced his march toward the capital. Rustam had in fact arrived at Hyderabad on the fourth accompanied by his nephews Nasir Khan and Mahomed Khan. The General's continued advance in spite of the Khairpur chiefs' arrival convinced the Hyderabad amirs of Napier's hostile intentions, and they sent summonses to several of their feudatories for men to defend the city.

Negotiations at Hyderabad had been arranged to open on February 6, but Outram, because of his late departure from Khairpur and the lack of transportation, did not reach Hyderabad until February 8. On the evening of his arrival he held a conference with all the amirs of Sind who, led by Nasir Khan of Hyderabad, referred to their adherence to former treaties and the failure of the British to do so. They demanded to see the so-called treasonable letters on which the treaty was based and which they denied having ever written. As Napier had used the seals on these letters as a means of positive identification, the amirs pointed out to Outram: "How easily seals are forged you yourself know having required us to punish one of our subjects who forged yours, when you resided here, two years ago." [38] Outram was hard put to refute these arguments, and, as the conference continued, two causes of conflict emerged as important—the replacement of Mir Rustam as *rais* of Upper Sind by Ali Murad and the General's continued advance on Hyderabad, which the amirs claimed was so arousing their Baluchis that the amirs feared they might not be able to control them.[39]

Outram did his best to make Napier halt. On February 8 he

99

ANNEXATION AND ITS REPERCUSSIONS

wrote that he expected no hostilities because the amirs had apparently not removed their women from Hyderabad. "I have promised them that I will beg of you to halt the Troops wherever this may meet you." [40] On the 11th he stated that he expected the Upper Sind amirs to sign the treaty and enclosed a scheme whereby the Khairpur amirs would not lose additional territory to Ali Murad as *rais*.[41] All amirs except Nasir Khan of Khairpur, who subsequently fled, having signed the treaty on the 12th, Outram wrote to Napier:

These fools are in the utmost alarm *in consequence of the continued progress of your troops towards Hyderabad, not withstanding their acceptance of the treaty which they hoped would have caused you to stop*—If you come beyond Hala (if, so far) I fear that they will be impelled by their fears to assemble their rabble with a view to defend themselves and their families in the idea that we are determined to destroy them, *not withstanding their submission.*[42]

On the evening of the same day he again wrote:

I wrote you this morning to say what a state of commotion they are in in the city at your continued advance after the Ameers had subscribed to the treaty. . . . I really wish *I was empowered to tell them positively that you do not propose bringing the troops beyond Hala if so far—as it is I can only express to them my hope that you will not do so now that they have complied with all our terms . . . I have great hope that you will have halted on receipt of my information that the Upper Scinde Ameers have also subscribed to the treaty.*[43]

The problem of Napier's continued advance centered on the capture of twenty-five armed Marri tribesmen intercepted by Jacob as they rode through his encampment on the 21st. A search revealed that some members of the group carried letters from Mir Mahomed Khan and Nasir Khan of Hyderabad asking

100

ANNEXATION AND ITS REPERCUSSIONS

them to bring their forces to Hyderabad.[44] Napier was convinced he was the victim of a vast plot. On February 7 he had received a letter from Nasir Khan of Hyderabad contending that the General had promised not to move from Shera until February 9 (which Napier denied),[45] while on the 10th Outram requested him to halt for a day because Rustam wished a postponement of the signing of the treaty until after the end of the Moslem festival of Moharum.[46] All this together with the fact that Gholam Shah, Nasir Khan's envoy empowered to treat with Outram, was also the agent deputed to deal with the Marris, prompted Napier to write to Ellenborough:

It is now plain that they wanted to delay till the 9th to get their people together. The 'Moharam' prevented this, because the chiefs could not get their followers to march while the religious festival lasted. This ended, off they started for the rendezvous at Meanee—twelve miles from Hyderabad; as all my information concurs in stating and as the arrest of the chiefs *proves* for they were preceded by several hundred of their men who passed in the night but off sight of Jacob's camp.

In these circumstances I mean to wait till I receive the signatures on the treaty; and then act towards the culprit Ameers as circumstances seem to demand, unless in the meantime, I receive further instructions from your Lordship. I expected when I ordered Jacob to arrest armed men that I should alight upon something to elucidate matters, but to catch as many chiefs, and so clear a letter was my good luck.[47]

The capture of the Marri chiefs was the last straw; Outram reported to Napier on the afternoon of the 13th that he had heard the Baluch *sirdars* had sworn to oppose the British unless Rustam was reinstated.[48] Later in the day he warned Napier of a possible attack on his troops although he deemed it unlikely,[49] because the large force which intelligence had reported at Kunhera in reality was just an escort for Rustam's women. The

101

ANNEXATION AND ITS REPERCUSSIONS

detachment had only six guns without ammunition or carriages, as these had been stolen by Ali Murad.[50] But on the 13th Napier wrote Outram:

I neither can nor will halt now. Their object is very clear and I will not be their dupe. I shall march to Hyderabad tomorrow and next to Halla and attack every body of armed men I meet. . . . If the treaty was not signed on the 12th according to their promise of the 11th when the Ameers, *knew that I had halted*; there can remain no doubt of the fact that they have been using every trick to get over the Moharrun, as they could no sooner collect their troops. . . . If men die in consequence of my delay their blood must be justly charged to my account.[51]

Actually the amirs had signed the treaty on the twelfth, and Napier had only halted because his men needed rest.[52]

By February 15 Napier must have known that all the amirs with the exception of Nasir Khan of Khairpur had subscribed to the treaty; yet he wrote to Outram:

Do not pledge yourself to anything whatever. I am in full march on Hyderabad and *will make no peace with the Ameers.* I will attack them instantly whenever I come up to their troops, they need send no proposals, the time has passed and I will not receive their messengers, there must be *no pledges made on any account.*[53]

Outram now felt that hostilities were inevitable. He wrote to the commanding officer of the 41st Regiment, *en route* to Karachi, to halt wherever he was; the General might have need of him;[54] he also warned the officer commanding in Karachi.[55] Mir Shahdad offered to come and reside in the British residency to insure Outram's safety but the commissioner refused to hear of it and informed Shahdad that if any of his men engaged in hostile actions against the British, he would be held responsible.[56] Outram also wrote to the Hyderabad durbar and urged

102

ANNEXATION AND ITS REPERCUSSIONS

the amirs that they should not engage in any hostile actions against the British, for if the Khairpur amirs were determined to court their own destruction, the Hyderabad durbar should convince them to return to their own territory and not aid them. If the Hyderabad amirs did this, Outram pledged that no harm would befall them.[57]

But Mirs Nasir Khan and Mahomed Khan had on this same day decided to commence hostilities, pressed as they were by their Baluchis, one of whom had presented Nasir Khan with a woman's dress.[58] Sobdar tried desperately to keep aloof for he was well aware of the fate likely to overtake his cousins, but his bellicose feudatories embroiled him without his leave.[59]

As Lambrick emphasizes, Napier's contention that the amirs had long planned hostile action against the British was disproved by the fact that no warlike preparations were being made in Hyderabad and that the court was spending all of its time preparing for the weddings of Mir Hussein Ali and Sobdar's son, Fateh Ali.[60] Nonetheless, the Baluchis could not be contained, and on the night of February 14 attacked the residency, which was defended by the light company of the 22d Regiment, a few Sepoys, and six British officers, including Outram and E. J. Brown. On the next day the defenders escaped with some difficulty on the steamers "Planet" and "Satellite," suffering casualties of three dead and ten wounded and bringing with them the agency records and some private property.[61]

The war in Sind was as short as it was sanguinary.[62] On February 17, at Miani, in a battle in which the British losses were sixty-three killed and those of the Baluchis were estimated as being between two and six thousand, Napier defeated the combined forces of Hyderabad, Khairpur, and Mirpur. Hyderabad was surrendered without a struggle and its considerable treasure turned over to the prize agents. The £70,000 Napier received as his share no doubt helped satisfy his appetite for rupees. On March 26 Sir Charles defeated Sher Mahomed of Mirpur, the only remaining chief of importance left in the

103

ANNEXATION AND ITS REPERCUSSIONS

field. On June 13, Jacob again won the day in an all but blood-less victory over Sher Mahomed at Shahdadpur,[63] and the annexation of Sind was formally announced in August.

Upon viewing the remains of the Baluchi dead at Miani Napier remarked that "the blood is on the Ameers, not on me." [64] But there seems little doubt that his assessment was less than accurate. When Outram wrote to Napier on February 12, explaining that the amirs had signed the treaties and urging that Napier should stop his advance, he also sent the notes of the conferences held with the amirs on February 8 and 12 for further transmission to the Governor-General. These notes contained the amirs' denial of guilt and the petition of Mir Rustam for reinstatement as *rais* of Upper Sind.[65] Napier promised: "I will state to Lord Ellenborough all the Ameers say because it is fair to them. . . . I will at once send Lord Ellenborough a copy of what passed." [66] Napier submitted neither the notes of the conferences nor Outram's letter to the Governor-General, but a copy of the notes finally reached Lord Fitzgerald, then president of the Board of Control, through Sir George Arthur to whom Outram had sent a set. When the Secret Committee asked Ellenborough why he had not sent the notes he could only reply: "I never heard of the existence of these notes till I read your letter today—I know absolutely nothing of what may have passed between Major Outram and the Ameers." [67] To Ellenborough's letter asking for information on the missing documents,[68] Napier could give no adequate reply.[69]

Sir Charles to a large extent condemned himself. In the dispatch he wrote after the battle of Miani he claimed that "on the 14th instant, the whole body of the Ameers, assembled in full durbar, formally affixed their seals to the draft Treaty." [70] This was a deliberate misrepresentation designed to excuse his bellicose actions between February 12 and 14, for it is certain that at the time of his writing Napier had in his possession several letters written by Outram giving the 12th as the date when the Amirs subscribed to the treaties.

104

ANNEXATION AND ITS REPERCUSSIONS

Ellenborough was soon faced with his mistake in confusing the two Nasir Khans but he blandly wrote to the Secret Committee:

I am unable to account satisfactorily for this error. . . . It is satisfactory however to know that Sir C. Napier was aware of the error, and that the letter inaccurately addressed to Meer Nuseer Khan of Khyrpore must have been delivered to Meer Nuseer Khan of Hyderabad to whom its contents applied.[71]

The extent of Ellenborough's delusion, his lack of information, and the mistake of having invested Sir Charles Napier with absolute power were now clear. Napier had indeed sent the letter to Nasir Khan of Hyderabad, but his cousin of Khairpur nonetheless suffered the penalty and was never informed why he had lost so much territory without reason.

The degree to which Ellenborough had strayed from his instructions and from his earlier declared policies was manifested by the tenor of communications from the Secret Committee. Fitzgerald had advised the Governor-General to be extremely careful and to avoid hostilities in Sind.[72] Ripon on June 3 (almost three months after the battle of Miani) had written Ellenborough that while he realized that views taken on the same matter might not always be identical when seen from different hemispheres, the Board of Control would earnestly press upon the Governor-General, "to avoid as much as possible *committing* us to any course affecting territorial possessions and extension." The board, he continued, would prefer to be "left more at liberty to form a previous decision as to what should be done, than one after the judgement of what has been done." [73]

It was of course much too late for such an admonition. Ellenborough, for his part, complained of the lack of instructions from home and of the consequent necessity of acting on his own initiative.[74] To which Peel replied:

105

ANNEXATION AND ITS REPERCUSSIONS

If a Governor General supposes that the Government at home has no responsibility for acts done in India—that in the absence of necessary information . . . that they have nothing to do but to ratify and approve. He is under a great misapprehension of our Duties and our relations to him.[75]

Gladstone later recalled that the entire Cabinet had been against the annexation of Sind.[76] But as Peel wrote, "Time—distance—the course of events may have so fettered our discretion that we [had] no alternative but to maintain [the] occupation of Scinde." [77]

While Ellenborough was entering the lists against the Secret Committee, Napier was appointed Governor of Sind. He promptly abolished slavery and duties on the river, the Indus being declared free for all nations.[78] To the "Beloochis of Scinde," he issued a proclamation couched in typical Naperian prose:

Your princes are prisoner; their capital and their Treasure are in my possession. You fought like men, but were defeated, and many of your chiefs slain. Master of Scinde I now address you in the words of reason, in hopes that I may not be obliged to shed more of your blood.

The Talpoors have fallen before the swords of the English as the Caloras fell before the swords of the Talpoors; so God has decreed it should be and so it is. The decrees of God are unchangeable. If you resist I will treat you harshly and drive you over the Indus. I have an abundance of soldiers. Thousands more will come; your blood will be shed. But if you are tranquil and return to your homes. Your Jaghires and possessions of all kinds shall be respected and the English be your friends. You will be happy.[79]

The Secret Committee was told that the "joy with which the inhabitants of Scinde view the change of masters is most gratifying," [80] and Napier wrote:

ANNEXATION AND ITS REPERCUSSIONS

Our revenues are improving. The sums I have set down for you are extracts taken from the office archives, and show a revenue of nearly thirty thousand pounds a month under all the draw-backs of war, locusts, pestilence, and ignorance of the sources of taxation and its proper amount. . . . But here is a net sum averaging twenty lacs or two hundred thousand stirling plus, surplus. Be assured that in ten years it may be doubled; but here are £360,000 revenue already, £300,000 being a clear surplus, after paying a civil government.[81]

These statements were a gross misrepresentation of the facts. Joseph Hume was closer to the truth when he pointed out in Commons that the annexation of Sind was now recoiling on the British in the shape of a heavy charge amounting to nearly £1,000,000 annually. Commercially Sind was of little use and the army of occupation numbered between thirteen and four-teen thousand men. In fact, the deficit in the revenue of India, Hume continued, had been solely produced by the expenses in-curred in Sind, for until its annexation there had always been a surplus in the Indian revenue and now the deficit amounted to £39,000,000.[82]

In England the annexation caused a strong negative reaction both in official and unofficial circles. It was the treatment of the deposed amirs that aroused particular resentment. They were handled quite indiscriminately, regardless of their degree of involvement in the hostilities, and were exiled to Calcutta. It was assumed by the Government of India that they would later reside in Mecca or Egypt. Not until 1855 were most of them, or rather their descendants, allowed to return to Sind.

The conduct of the British Indian Government toward the amirs was the prime irritant to both Ellenborough's supporters and foes in London. On July 6, Ripon, now chairman of the Board of Control, wrote to the Governor-General:

The justice of the entire deprivation of the Ameers and their expulsion from Scinde is questioned and the plan of keeping the

107

ANNEXATION AND ITS REPERCUSSIONS

Country is condemned as expensive and impolitic; inconsistent with former declarations; and after all uncertain in its issue.[83]

Again, on December 4, he wrote to Ellenborough that the treatment of the amirs was stirring up trouble at home and could they not be treated more liberally and indulgently.[84] Ellenborough replied that the return of the amirs to Sind would weaken the British position on the Indus and would "ultimately lead to another unnecessary contest for a country now subdued." [85] Besides, restoration of the amirs would remove the moral effect of the punishment of these treacherous princes, and the return of their lands would only make them a rallying point for opposition to British rule. Regarding Ripon's suggestions that the guilt or innocence of each amir should be judged individually, the Governor-General wrote:

How vain would it be to seek this absolute perfection of justice in the treatment of Princes convicted of Treachery and subdued in War. Their treatment must be governed by other principles than those which may be observed in the treatment of common men. It must be governed by enlarged views of National policy; and the compassion we may feel for the individuals, however innocent and even laudable its exercise, were private interests alone involved, must not be permitted to affect the adoption of measures essential to the welfare of the people we have redeemed and the state we serve.[86]

But Ellenborough's views were not well received, and Napier was only supported by military figures such as the Duke of Wellington (for militarily the Sind campaign had been most expertly handled) and by his legion of kinsmen, including his brother, Sir William Napier, then Governor of Guernsey, who was destined to write a long apology for Sir Charles. *The Times* of May 6, 1843, strongly attacked Ellenborough, contrasting his pacific proclamation of the previous October with his more recent actions. It blamed him for replacing Outram with Napier

108

ANNEXATION AND ITS REPERCUSSIONS

and condemned his "indistinct charges, one-sided judgement, irritating sentence, summary execution, and finally ruinous and hasty penalty on resistance." The *Edinburgh Review* of April, 1844, was also severely critical of the Sind policy.[87]

The chief attack in Commons came from a member of the Tory party itself—the noted philanthropist, Lord Ashley.[88] He wondered why the amirs were never confronted with the so-called treasonable letters and why, if the amirs were planning to fight, they had made no preparations to move their families or their treasure. It seemed curious to him that the amirs should have failed to attack while British fortunes were at their lowest ebb in Afghanistan and then have become actively hostile once the Company's strength was renewed. Ashley moved that the amirs be restored to their rights and possessions.[89] Lord Jocelyn, also a Tory, supported Ashley, strongly criticized the culpable conduct of Ellenborough in regard to Sind, and questioned the advisability of having annexed the province. Lord Ashley's motion was opposed by the radical Roebuck, who was mainly interested in vindicating Napier at the expense of Auckland, and by Commodore Napier, who came to the defense of his relation, Charles.[90]

Peel, although he felt that "the treatment of the Ameers is really disgraceful to the character of this Country," [91] and was, as we have already seen, opposed to the annexation, nonetheless was forced by the exigencies of the situation and the plight of his party, to defend Ellenborough's actions in Sind. He referred to "some great principle at work wherever civilization and refinement came in contact with barbarism, which makes it impossible to apply the rules observed amongst civilized nations." [92] The Prime Minister thought Ashley's motion ill-advised, as the restoration of the amirs to their estates or their indemnification would place an excessive strain on the revenues of Sind.[93] Ashley in rebuttal claimed that none of the points he had raised had been answered, but the House duly divided for the Government (164 to 9, with many abstentions). After a

ANNEXATION AND ITS REPERCUSSIONS

heated debate on the subject of a vote of thanks to the army in Sind the matter was not raised again in Westminster for some time.[94]

While the storm was mild in Parliament, it soon became intense in the General Court of Directors of the East India Company. On November 17, 1843, a General Court of Proprietors met and a resolution was entered by eight proprietors, including W. J. Eastwick and Joseph Hume, which stated:

1. . . . that, from the printed papers recently laid before Parliament on the subject of Scinde, it is the opinion of this Court that the proceedings of the Government of India, which ended in the dethronement, exile, and imprisonment of the Ameers, and the seizure of their country, were un-called for, impolitic and unjust.

2. That this Court, does, therefore, most earnestly recommend to the Court of Directors the immediate adoption of such steps, by Representation to her Majesty's Government or otherwise as may cause all practicable reparation to be made for the injustice already committed, and enforce the abandonment of a line of policy inconsistent with good faith and subversive of the interests of the British rule in India.[95]

A similar motion was entered on January 26, 1844,[96] but under pressure from the Government, and after an acrimonious debate both resolutions were withdrawn on February 21. But the matter remained an open wound until finally, in April, 1844, under the prerogatives granted it by the Act of 1783, the court recalled Lord Ellenborough as Governor-General of India. Although the official reasons given for this action were insubordination and the Governor-General's excessive absence from the Bengal presidency, the real motivation was the annexation of Sind against the Company's will and the heavy expense thereby incurred.[97]

110

Sir Charles Napier's light flickered out more slowly. He served as Governor of Sind until 1847, when he returned to England and retirement. The disastrous early stages of the Sikh war caused his appointment, amidst much public acclaim, as commander in chief of the British forces in India. However, by the time he arrived in Bombay in May, 1849, Lord Gough had already put out the last sparks of Sikh resistance, and Napier remained only long enough to engage in some petty squabbles with Lord Dalhousie. Sir Charles's final departure from India took place on February 3, 1851. The old warrior lived only two more years; he died in 1853 at the age of seventy-one—to this day a controversial figure.

The long paper battle between Napier and Outram over the justice of the annexation of Sind was to end in favor of the latter. In 1845, Sheik Ali Hussein, the chief minister of Ali Murad, quarreled with his master and was discharged. The bond of allegiance between the two now being dissolved, the Sheik hinted in some detail that both the Treaty of Nunahar as it existed and Rustam's abdication document were forgeries. It soon came to light that a box supposedly containing the Nunahar treaty and other documents had disappeared from the British residency in Hyderabad and that another box containing English translations of these same papers had been stolen. Napier had decided (it must be said in fairness) that the past conduct of Mir Ali Murad had to be investigated thoroughly; but, as he was about to leave Sind, he left only a rough memorandum on the matter with his assistant, Brown, to be shown to the General's successor.[98]

Sir George Clerk, the Governor of Bombay, subsequently examined Napier's memorandum and ordered a complete investigation, which, if it proved Ali Murad's guilt, would necessitate his deposal and the annexation of his lands by the British; while at the same time were Ali Murad convicted, the other Talpurs, now in captivity, might be restored to the right bank of the Indus. Lord Dalhousie, the Governor-General, decided that no

111

ANNEXATION AND ITS REPERCUSSIONS

steps should be taken against Ali Murad unless his complicity could be established in an open inquiry. In other words, in Lambrick's view, he was to have the very rights which Ellenborough and Napier had denied his relations in 1843.[99]

A commission was appointed and sat for about two weeks in April, 1850. During its sessions it was conclusively proved not only that the existing copy of the Treaty of Nunahar was a forgery but, more important, that Rustam's resignation of the Turban was also a fabrication. The latter agreement between Ali Murad and Mir Rustam had been signed at Kot Diji on December 20, 1842. Rustam had indeed abdicated in favor of Ali Murad and had relinquished his own personal territories to facilitate the negotiations with the British. But he had made four conditions: Ali Murad was not to annex the territory north of Rohri, because it had been ceded to the British; Ali Murad was to renounce all claims to the lands of Rustam's sons and to those of the sons of Mir Mubarak; Ali Murad was to support in an appropriate style Rustam, his family, attendants, male and female slaves; and the former *rais* was to retain possession of Khairpur itself for the rest of his life.[100] Ali Murad had embodied all this in the treaty and signed it, undertaking not to "encroach a single hair on what I have written, as God is my witness." [101] This document, when dispatched to Napier along with Rustam's letter, was intercepted by Sheik Ali Hussein (who with remarkable perspicacity preserved it), and the forged version was sent to the General in its place.[102]

Ali Murad's guilt now being proved, he was deposed, his territories annexed by the British, and the way cleared for the return of the remaining Talpurs to Sind in 1855—not as princes in their own right but as pensioners of the Crown.[103]

7. Conclusion

THE HISTORY of Anglo-Sind intercourse tends to reinforce the impression common to many students of the British Empire that governmental policy toward the imperial domain and toward areas contiguous to British possessions was seldom characterized by consistency. This is not to say that British governments differed in their position when faced with certain recurring situations such as the threat of foreign invasion or the desirability of establishing profitable trade connections when feasible, but rather that British actions and attitudes changed with circumstances and that circumstances varied from area to area.

Early contacts with Sind were limited initially to trading establishments and then to treaties which had as their sole purpose the protection of India from invasion first by France and later by Russia through the Indus valley. When these fears waned British interest in Sind faded. The Khosa raids on Cutch again brought the Company's agents to Sind. But the promulgation of an agreement in 1820 to protect the British and the *rao* of Cutch from further incursions by these predatory tribes reëstablished the earlier attitude of indifference toward Sind.

The mission of Dr. James Burnes to the Court of Hyderabad cast an entirely new light on Sind and more particularly on the Indus. As a result of Burnes's report of his journey, Sind was no longer considered an arid waste watered by a useless river but the highroad to Central Asia and the key to its trade. At last the cumbersome Ganges supply line to the British northwestern provinces could be replaced by a more efficient route—the Indus. That the river was not navigable was hardly even

113

CONCLUSION

considered and was not really recognized until after annexation.

By 1830, therefore, British interest in Sind had returned to the original motivation, that of commerce—not trade with Sind itself but with the interior of Asia where the Russians were already entrenched. Sind was to be a buffer against Russian attack and the Indus a major line of communication.

Slowly but surely British preponderance increased. At first British vessels were only tolerated on the river and a toll was levied on all shipping. Soon the Company was there by right and all duties were removed. Treaties in 1832, 1834, and 1838–1839 changed the amirs from the rulers of an independent nation to princes of a client state. The Afghan war only added to their degradation. The provisions of former treaties were abrogated, their possessions were seized, and British troops marched through the Bolan Pass to restore Shah Shuja to the throne of his forefathers.

Despite the humiliations heaped on the amirs and the steady expansion of British influence, it has been pointed out that the absorption of Sind into British India was not desired by responsible officials either in London or in Calcutta. In the final analysis it was not calculated Government policy which determined the course of Anglo-Sind relations but the curious interplay between the personalities of Ellenborough and Napier, with Outram acting as a catalyst. Napier's sixty years of frustration and Ellenborough's latent megalomania were able, in an era of slow communications, to carry the day against the combined weight of the East India Company and the British Government.

There are several reasons why inconsistencies in colonial policy occurred. Frequently they were caused by the conflicting interests of the home authorities (dedicated to financial stability) and the colonial official (concerned with the immediate problems of order and security). Of course a new governor-general or subordinate official, by altering the policies of his predecessor, might contribute to this impression of vacillation which so confused the native rules of India. Thus Sobdar, whom

CONCLUSION

the British had considered their dedicated enemy before 1838, turned into their favorite after that date, because of the happy accident of his being a Sunni rather than a Shia, only to be treated with the same severity as his brethren after the battle of Miani. The institution of *rais* of Lower Sind was destroyed by Auckland, who guaranteed each chief in his possession independently, but Ellenborough would have restored the *rais* had the war not intervened. Rustam, the darling of Alexander Burnes, was considered a villain by Napier, and Ali Murad, whom Pottinger thought to be an underhanded rogue,[1] was judged the most dependable of all the amirs by the General.

The outlook of governors-general often changed during their term of office. In the case of Ellenborough, one must conclude that he sincerely believed when he assumed office, "that the further extension of its dominions forms no part of the policy of the British Government," [2] and that circumstances, however he might have misinterpreted them, forced him to change his views. Communications were still so slow that the Board of Control because of faulty information was frequently in disagreement with the Governor-General; although it might be that the home authorities, had they been completely informed, would still have disapproved of Ellenborough's actions.

Upon occasion the Board and the Company urged expansion over the objections of the Governor-General. Auckland wrote to Hobhouse: "I am always a little surprised at your warlike tone in regard to Lahore and I shall find it more difficult, than you seem to think it would be, to frame a declaration of war against the Sikhs." [3]

Sometimes the home authorities and the Governor-General agreed on what course to follow—for example, when both Palmerston and Hobhouse urged Auckland on the bellicose course which led to the Afghan war. But these instances, because of the difference in the quantity and accuracy of the information available at the two levels, were infrequent. At the beginning of the century it usually took two and a half years to

115

CONCLUSION

receive a reply to a letter sent from India to England. The use of the Red Sea route cut this period to a year in the 1840's and occasionally even to as little as three months—still an extremely long interval in a time of crisis when new developments arose daily if not hourly. The letter ordering Lord Ellenborough to avoid hostilities in Sind at all costs arrived three months after the battle of Miani.

But the problem of slow communications was not limited to intercourse between England and India, for if the home government was fettered by the lack of up-to-date information, so was the Governor-General. Three weeks usually elapsed between the despatch of a letter to Sind and the receipt of a reply. Ellenborough complained to Wellington in 1843 regarding his correspondence with Sir Charles Napier that "even when I was at Ferozepore, it took twelve days to receive an answer from him and no time was to be lost." [4] On February 26, 1843, eleven days after the battle of Miani, Sir George Arthur wrote to Ellenborough:

The great difficulty I feel is the total want of official information from Scinde and I sometimes fear that, if any extensive outbreak were to occur, the troops might be seriously compromised before we received such trustworthy intelligence as would justify our taking any important steps toward assisting them. [5]

Hence before the advent of the telegraph, primitive communications and the often sporadic and inaccurate information received frequently left the Governor-General at the mercy of his subordinates in the provinces. It made the ruling of India from England both a folly and a delusion, and provincial officials were given a greater importance than their positions merited, often to the detriment of the native rulers. Certainly slow communications and the great trust the Governor-General reposed in Napier made him virtually a power unto himself, and

CONCLUSION

allowed events to proceed toward the hostilities that were to make the name of Sir Charles Napier a household word and to lead to the erection of his statue next to that of Nelson in Trafalgar Square.

As British officers in India were largely unhampered by administrative restraints, the attitude they maintained toward the native peoples is of some importance. Most British officers did not consider the Indians their peers nor, as Sir Robert Peel stated in Parliament, did they feel that the rules which governed the intercourse between civilized nations applied to barbarians.[6] Thus, any action would be legitimate if it could be justified as being in the British national interest, and Ellenborough wrote that it would be vain to seek the absolute perfection of justice in dealing with the amirs.[7] The intensity of this attitude varied from individual to individual but it was evident to some degree in virtually every officer who acted on behalf of the Company on the subcontinent. Pottinger, despite his opposition to the retention of Karachi and his criticism of Napier[8] after the annexation, was unvaryingly inimical to the amirs. Outram would certainly seem to be an exception, but even the "Bayard of India" was not above stooping to subterfuge in attempting to prove the authenticity of the "treasonable" letter Mir Rustam was accused of having sent to Maharajah Sher Singh of Lahore.[9]

Nevertheless British officials in nineteenth-century India frequently expressed the conviction that they held a mandate to bring the benefits of Western civilization to the backward peoples of Asia. As A. P. Thornton so aptly puts it, the term "oriental government" merely invoked visions of depravity and despotism to the majority of Englishmen. To them no "oriental" state was capable of a beneficent existence. That it often fulfilled the needs of its subjects seemed beyond the point. The sincere imperialist of the nineteenth century was a missionary for Western civilization, and to him, Thornton points out, "good government was better than self-government."[10] In this light the acquisition of colonial possessions and their enlightened rule

117

CONCLUSION

was the duty of every civilized nation. Nehru in his autobiography recalls:

There was something fascinating about the British approach to the Indian problem, even though it was singularly irritating. The calm assurance of always being right and having borne a great burden worthily, faith in their racial destiny and their own brand of imperialism, contempt and anger at the unbelievers and sinners, who challenged the foundations of the true faith— there was something of a religious temper about this attitude. Like the Inquisitors of old, they were bent on saving us regardless of our desires in the matter.[11]

Undoubtedly this sentiment, though often sincere, was frequently merely a rationalization for territorial aggrandizement. But regardless, it placed the British in a philosophical dilemma from which they could not easily extricate themselves. Were they honor bound to respect indigenous Indian customs as the Company had done in the early years of its rule? Or should they judge Indian mores by Western European standards? It is generally acknowledged that Bentinck's edict prohibiting *sati* did more to arouse Indian antipathy than decades of economic exploitation. When Napier received a petition to allow *sati* in Sind he wrote: "You say *suttee* is the custom. Well we too have a custom which is to hang men who burn women alive. You build your funeral pyre and I will build my gallows beside it, and let each of us act according to custom." [12]

Most British officers serving in Sind agreed with Crow's statement that the Sindians had "acquired the vices both of barbarity on one side and civilization on the other without the virtues of either." [13] On the other hand, W. J. Eastwick considered that the amirs' subjects were "peaceful and contented and that their condition might bear advantageous comparison with that of the people of many of our own provinces." The amirs, he continued, were liberal and forbearing and were always accessible to even the lowliest subject.[14] Lambrick states that

118

CONCLUSION

although Sind was an Islamic autocracy it was in practice much less despotic than the governments of most neighboring states.[15]

It would be unfair not to give credit to the considerable army of able administrators who, although they might not have achieved their posts through open examination, nonetheless did a highly creditable job, dedicating a lifetime to the Company or the Crown—often in the most difficult circumstances—without the hope of great recompense. Men such as Outram and Metcalfe were distinguished, devoted public servants, bearing comparison with the best in any era of imperial history. A myriad of others, whose attitudes to the native governments were not above reproach, once the British took control found the improvement of the physical conditions of life and the enriching of the area through public works compatible with their duties and their concept of the civilizing process inherent in the British *raj*. This was true of Whitehall as well, for if it was characteristic of British rule in India and elsewhere that regions were frequently annexed against the wishes of London, it was equally true that the British authorities inevitably accepted the *fait accompli* and did their utmost to introduce the attributes of Western civilization as they saw them. Thus Sind in the years following its addition to India was metamorphosed at great expense, and many of the early improvements were instituted by the erstwhile conqueror, Sir Charles Napier. A revised system of laws was promulgated, banditry stamped out, the excellent harbor at Karachi built, a complex system of canals and dams to irrigate the fertile lands of the Indus Valley constructed, and railways slowly advanced to connect one part of Sind with another. By the time of the British exodus in 1947 Sind was a rich agricultural area and Karachi sufficiently developed to become the capital and chief port of the new nation of Pakistan. Nevertheless, British Indian officers were on the whole afflicted with a decidedly myopic outlook which, at least in the nineteenth century, was no doubt in part due to the short shrift often given to colonial appointments by the British Government.

119

CONCLUSION

Although this accusation cannot be applied to Indian civil appointments, which usually received careful consideration, the military lists were less scrupulously drawn up, and certainly the appointment of Napier to the command in Sind was open to criticism, achieved as it was through the political influence of his brother William. The whole system of nineteenth-century colonial appointments was described by James Mill as a vast system of outdoor relief for the upper classes, and there was some justice in George Cornwall Lewis' claim that "the scum of England is poured into the colonies; briefless barristers, broken down merchants, ruined debauchees, the offal of every calling and profession are crammed into colonial places." [16]

These then were the main factors that governed the East India Company's intercourse with the amirs of Sind—commercial interest, considerations of defense and security, and the character and power of the ambitious "man on the spot" in an era of slow communications. They were to reappear on continents and in places far removed from the valley of the Indus.

Notes

ABBREVIATIONS

Auckland Papers—British Museum, London

Bengal Secret Letters—Secret letters from the Government of Bengal to the Secret Committee of the Court of Directors of the East India Company.

BGR—Bombay Government Records, Elphinstone College, Bombay

Board's Secret Drafts—The Board of Control's drafts of secret letters to be sent to India.

Broughton Papers—British Museum, London

Ellenborough Papers—British Museum, London

Hobhouse Papers—India Office Library and British Museum, London

Indian Secret Letters—Secret letters from the Secret Committee of the Court of Directors of the East India Company to the Government of India.

IOR—India Office Library Records, India Office Library, London

NAI—National Archives of India Records, National Archives of India, New Delhi

Napier Papers—British Museum, London

Peel Papers—British Museum, London

PGR—Punjab Government Records, Lahore, West Pakistan

Ripon Papers—British Museum, London

SC—*Correspondence Relative to Sind, 1838–1843*, Presented to both Houses of Parliament, by Command of Her Majesty (London: T. R. Harrison, 1843).

SSC—*Correspondence Relative to Sinde, Supplementary to the Papers presented to Parliament in 1843*, Presented to both Houses of Parliament, by Command of Her Majesty (London: T. R. Harrison, 1844).

NOTES TO PREFACE
(Pp. vii–ix)

[1] There was no telegraph in 1843 on which Napier could have sent the message. The anecdote probably originated in a *Punch* cartoon of 1844 although Napier once used a similar phrase in his diary.

[2] Quoted by S. P. Chablani, *Economic Conditions in Sind, 1592–1843*, p. 76.

[3] For excellent descriptions of the post-1784 system of Indian government, see C. H. Philips, *The East India Company, 1784–1834*, A. H. Imlah, *Lord Ellenborough*, and B. B. Misra, *The Central Administration of the East India Company 1773–1834*.

[4] The three younger brothers were Mir Ghulamali Khan, Mir Karam Ali Khan, and Mir Murad Ali Khan. The four amirs were collectively known as the *Char-Yar*—the four friends. The various Talpur governments of Sind were family corporations including a number of amirs of various ranks who usually ruled under the guidance of a chief. In this case four amirs acting together were the ultimate power.

NOTES TO CHAPTER 1
(Pp. 1–12)

[1] See J. Lee Schneidman, "The Proposed Invasion of India by Russia and France in 1801," *Journal of Indian History*, XXXV:2 (Aug. 1957), 167–175.

[2] Sind was under the immediate jurisdiction of the Bombay Presidency.

[3] IOR, *Selections from the Records of the Commissioner in Sind*, file 203, p. 500.

[4] *Ibid.*

[5] *Ibid.*

[6] IOR, *Home and Miscellaneous Series*, Vol. 333 (24), pp. 393–449, Crow to Duncan, May 7, 1800.

[7] See C. U. Aitchison, *A Collection of Treaties, Engagements and Sanads*, VIII, 311–317, for orders issued to this effect by Mir Fatehali Kahn.

123

NOTES

[8] One lakh equals Rs. 100,000 or £10,000 at the exchange rate prevailing at that time.

[9] IOR, *Home and Miscellaneous Series*, Vol. 333 (24), pp. 393–449, Crow to Duncan, May 7, 1800.

[10] *Ibid.*

[11] *Ibid.*, pp. 507–511, Aga Abdul Hussein to Crow, Aug. 12, 1800.

[12] *Ibid.*, pp. 503–507, Mirza Mahomed Ishmael to Crow, Aug. 10, 1800.

[13] *Ibid.*, pp. 502–503, Fatehali to Crow, Aug. 12, 1800.

[14] For the text of Zaman Shah's letter see C. L. Mariwalla, "British Adventure in Sind," *Journal of the Sind Historical Society*, I (June, 1942).

[15] IOR, *Home and Miscellaneous Series*, Vol. 333 (24), pp. 557–561, Duncan to Wellesley, Nov. 19, 1800.

[16] BGR, *Secret and Political Department Diaries*, No. 165, Abdul Hussein Bobhanee in a letter of Jan. 6, 1805, wrote that all Sind was afraid of the Afghan king and wanted to reëstablish amicable relations with the British. Zaman Shah was supposedly only four stages from Shikarpur.

[17] NAI, *Original Consultations*, No. 1, March 14, 1809.

[18] Gilbert Elliot, *Life and Letters of Gilbert Elliot, First Earl of Minto, from 1807–1841, While Governor-General of India*, p. 51, Minto to Colonel Bray, Oct. 11, 1807.

[19] IOR, *Board's Secret Drafts*, March 2, 1808.

[20] IOR, *Bengal Secret and Separate Branch Consultations*, February 29, 1805, N. H. Smith (Bushire) to Edmonstone (secretary to the Central Government), Jan. 17, 1808.

[21] NAI, Foreign Department, *Secret and Separate Branch Proceedings*, Aug. 8, 1808, No. 5.

[22] IOR, *Bengal Secret and Separate Branch Consultations*, March 14, 1808, No. 1, Minto in Council to Duncan, March 14, 1808.

[23] *Ibid.*

[24] *Ibid.*, May 30, 1808, No. 12, Duncan in Council (Bombay) to Minto, April 30, 1808.

[25] *Ibid.*, No. 14, Warden to Seton, April 30, 1808.

[26] IOR, *Bengal Secret and Separate Branch Proceedings*, December 5, 1808, No. 20, Seton to General Malcolm, Aug. 21, 1808.

[27] A *baylarbey* was a provincial governor.

[28] IOR, *Bengal Secret and Separate Branch Proceedings*, Dec. 5,

NOTES

1808, No. 20, Seton to General Malcolm, Aug. 24, 1808.

[29] *Ibid.*

[30] *Ibid.*, Oct. 3, 1808, No. 8, Seton to Duncan, July 24, 1808.

[31] Aitchison, *op. cit.*, VIII, 292–293, Aug. 18, 1808.

[32] IOR, *Secret and Political Branch Proceedings*, Jan. 23, 1809, No. 65, Seton to Duncan, Dec. 22, 1808.

[33] IOR, *Bengal Secret and Separate Branch Proceedings*, No. 17, Dec. 5, 1808, Seton to Shah Shuja, no date.

[34] BGR, *Secret and Political Department Diaries*, No. 248, Walker (Baroda) to Bombay, Sept. 24, 1808.

[35] IOR, *Bengal Secret and Separate Branch Proceedings*, Oct. 3, No. 7, Duncan to Minto, Oct. 1, 1808, No. 9, Warden (Bombay) to Seton, Sept. 1, 1808. *Board's Secret Drafts*, Oct. 2, 1809.

[36] IOR, *Bengal Secret and Separate Branch Proceedings*, No. 6, Minto to Duncan, Oct. 10, 1808.

[37] *Ibid.*, Dec. 5, 1808, No. 32.

[38] IOR, *Bengal Secret and Political Branch Consultations*, Feb. 6, 1809, No. 65, Seton to Duncan, Oct. 22, 1809.

[39] Sir Harford Jones to Persia; M. Elphinstone to Kabul; C. Metcalfe to Lahore.

[40] Duncan pointed this out to Minto. IOR, *Bengal Secret and Political Branch Consultations*, Jan. 23, 1809, No. 131, Duncan to Minto, Jan. 15, 1809.

[41] IOR, *Bengal Secret and Separate Branch Proceedings*, Oct. 10, 1808, No. 6, Minto to Duncan, Oct. 10, 1808.

[42] *Ibid.*, No. 7, Minto to Ghulamali Khan, Oct. 10, 1808.

[43] IOR, *Bengal Secret and Political Branch Consultations*, Jan. 2, 1809, No. 21, Duncan to Ghulamali Khan, Dec. 5, 1808.

[44] IOR, *Home and Miscellaneous Series*, Vol. 591, p. 201, Edmonstone to Smith, Nov. 28, 1808.

[45] *Ibid.*

[46] *Ibid.*, pp. 359–381, Smith to Edmonstone, Oct. 1, 1809.

[47] *Ibid.*

[48] *Ibid.*

[49] *Ibid.*

[50] *Ibid.*

[51] BGR, *Political Department Diaries*, Nov. 3 to 10, 1809, No. 345, Smith to Lieutenant-Colonel Walker, Resident in Cutch, Sept. 4, 1809.

NOTES

[52] IOR, *Home and Miscellaneous Series*, Vol. 591, pp. 359–381, Smith to Edmonstone, Oct. 10, 1809.

[53] Aitchison, *op. cit.* (note 7, above), VIII, 317.

[54] IOR, *Board's Secret Drafts*, June 29, 1810.

NOTES TO CHAPTER 2
(Pp. 13–29)

[1] NAI, Foreign Department, *Secret and Political Branch Proceedings*, No. 133, Nov. 28, 1802. Proposed agreement between Captain David Seton and the rajah of Cutch. It provided for advantages for British traders and for the suppression of pirates with the possible establishment of a British base for this purpose.

[2] BGR, *Secret Department Diaries*, No. 285, Sir Evan Napean in Council to the Governor-General, Feb. 3, 1814.

[3] *Ibid.*, Moira to Elphinstone, April 1, 1814.

[4] NAI, Foreign Department, *Secret Consultations*, Dec. 6, 1814, H. Babington (secretary to the Bombay Government) to Captain J. R. Carnac (Baroda), Nov. 7, 1814.

[5] BGR, *Secret Department Diaries*, No. 485 (5), Mirza Ismael Shah to M. Elphinstone, Proceedings, June 7, 1820.

[6] *Ibid.*, J. Henderson (Bombay Government) to Mirza Ismael Shah, June 1, 1820.

[7] IOR, *Bengal Secret and Political Proceedings*, July 22, 1820, No. 4, F. Warden to the Secretary of the Secret and Political Department (C. Metcalfe), June 10, 1820.

[8] *Ibid.*

[9] The title of the ruler of Cutch.

[10] NAI, Foreign Department, *Secret Consultations*, July 22, 1820, Elphinstone to Metcalfe, June 18, 1820.

[11] *Ibid.*

[12] *Ibid.*, Sept. 9, 1820, Warden to Metcalfe, Aug. 2, 1820.

[13] IOR, *Bengal Secret and Political Proceedings*, July 29, 1820, No. 9, Moira in Council to Warden, July 29, 1820.

[14] *Ibid.*

[15] *Ibid.*, Oct. 7, 1820, No. 2, Metcalfe to Warden, Oct. 7, 1820.

[16] *Ibid.*

[17] NAI, Foreign Department, *Secret Consultations*, Warden to Acting Resident James Williams (Cutch), Sept. 23, 1820.

126

NOTES

[18] C. U. Aitchison, A *Collection of Treaties, Engagements and Sanads*, VIII, 318.

[19] IOR, *Bengal Secret and Political Consultations*, Feb. 16, 1821, No. 3, Warden to Metcalfe, Nov. 11, 1820.

[20] *Ibid.*, No. 4, Warden to Metcalfe, Nov. 13, 1820.

[21] *Ibid.*, No. 7, Warden to Captain Saddler, Nov. 18, 1820.

[22] IOR, *Board's Secret Drafts*, March 10, 1824, to Amherst in Council.

[23] Edward Law (Lord Ellenborough), A *Political Diary 1828–1830*, II, 92.

[24] Lieutenant Colonel DeLacey Evans, *On the Designs of Russia.*

[25] Edward Law, *op. cit.*, II, 123.

[26] James Burnes, A *Narrative of a Visit to the Court of Sinde*, p. 120.

[27] Respectively, the locations of the Board of Control and of the East India Company.

[28] Edward Law, *op. cit.*, II, 144.

[29] *Ibid.*, pp. 150, 153.

[30] *Ibid.*

[31] Wm. Astall to Bentinck, Jan. 20, 1829, *Bentinck Papers.*

[32] IOR, *Board's Secret Drafts*, No. 185, Jan. 9, 1829.

[33] *Ibid.*, No. 208, Jan. 12, 1830.

[34] *Ibid.*

[35] IOR, *Bengal Secret and Political Consultations*, Dec. 31, 1830, No. 7, C. Norris to Burnes, Dec. 4, 1830.

[36] *Ibid.*, Oct. 14, 1830, No. 4, Minute by J. Malcolm (Governor of Bombay), Aug. 9, 1830.

[37] IOR, *Bengal Secret Letters*, Oct. 30, 1830, No. 113, Minute by Sir Charles Metcaife.

[38] *Ibid.*, May 6, 1831, Burnes to Pottinger, Feb. 23, 1831, quoted in Encl. No. 25, Pottinger to Secret Department, Bombay, Feb. 27, 1831.

[39] *Ibid.*, May 6, 1831, Encl. No. 29, Pottinger to Chief Secretary, Bombay (C. Norris), March 20, 1831.

[40] A holy man—a descendant of the Prophet.

[41] Alexander Burnes, A *Voyage on the Indus*, pp. 37–38.

[42] IOR, *Bengal Secret and Political Proceedings*, No. 21, Nov. 25, 1831.

[43] *Ibid.*, Sept. 9, 1831, No. 6, Pottinger to Bombay, July 7, 1831.

NOTES

[44] IOR, *Bengal Secret Letters,* Dec. 9, 1831, Encl. 35, Bengal Govt. to Clare, Oct. 22, 1831.

[45] *Ibid.*

[46] NAI, Foreign Department, *Secret Consultations,* Oct. 29, 1831, Prinsep to Pottinger, Oct. 22, 1831.

[47] IOR, *Indian Secret Letters,* July 2, 1832, Encl. 11, Pottinger to Governor- General, Feb. 5, 1832.

[48] *Ibid.,* July 2, 1832, Encl. 8, Pottinger to Governor-General, Feb. 3, 1832.

[49] *Ibid.,* Encl. 23, Pottinger to Prinsep, April 6, 1832.

[50] *Ibid.*

[51] *Ibid.*

[52] *Ibid.,* Encl. 24, Pottinger to Prinsep, April 14, 1832.

[53] *Ibid.*

[54] IOR, *Indian Secret Letters,* July 2, 1832.

[55] *Ibid.*

[56] *Ibid.*

[57] Aitchison, *op. cit.,* VIII, 320–321.

[58] *Ibid.*

[59] *Ibid.*

[60] Clare to Bentinck, March 10, 1832, *Bentinck Papers.*

[61] IOR, *Indian Secret Letters,* Dec. 28, 1832, Encl., Governor-General's Minute of June 8, 1832.

[62] *Ibid.*

[63] *Ibid.,* June 15, 1833.

[64] IOR, *Bengal Secret and Political Consultations,* Oct. 10, 1833, No. 13, remarks on the Indus tariff by H. Pottinger, July 4, 1833.

[65] *Ibid.,* No. 14, Bentinck to Pottinger, Oct. 10, 1833.

[66] *Ibid.*

[67] *Ibid.,* July 18, 1834, No. 2, Pottinger to Government, June 20, 1834.

[68] *Ibid.,* Sept. 5, 1834, No. 1, Pottinger to Macnaghten, Aug. 10, 1834.

[69] *Ibid.,* May 29, 1834, Encl. 14, Pottinger to Nur Mahomed, April 9, 1834.

[70] *Ibid.,* Sept. 24, 1834, No. 2, Macnaghten to Pottinger, Encl. No. 2, Sept. 5, 1834.

[71] IOR, *Indian Secret Letters,* March 5, 1835.

[72] Aitchison, *op. cit.,* VIII, 322–323.

NOTES

NOTES TO CHAPTER 3
(Pp. 30–42)

[1] Pottinger was in the curious position of being under the jurisdiction of the Bombay Government as resident in Cutch and under the control of the Central Government in his capacity as envoy to Sind.

[2] NAI, Foreign Department, *Political Consultations*, Jan. 11, 1836, Dr. J. F. Heddle to Burnes, Nov. 24, 1835.

[3] *Ibid.*, Burnes to Pottinger, Dec. 7, 1835, Pottinger to Bombay, Dec. 17, 1835.

[4] *Ibid.*, March 28, 1836, Bombay to India, Feb. 29, 1836.

[5] *Ibid.*, May 30, 1836, Nathan to Government, May 5, 1835.

[6] H. T. Lambrick, *Sir Charles Napier and Sind*, pp. 28–29.

[7] IOR, *Indian Secret Letters*, Sept. 26, 1836, Encl. 7, Macnaghten to Bombay, June 20, 1836.

[8] Auckland to Carnac, Aug. 5, 1836, *Auckland Papers*, No. 37689.

[9] *Ibid.*

[10] This was done on the assumption, by the British, that they were the heirs of the Marathas and hence had a right to the territory.

[11] This was the same theory used by the British in claiming the Cis-Sutlej territories as heirs to the Marathas.

[12] IOR, *Indian Secret Letters*, Sept. 26, 1836, Encl. 21, Macnaghten's instructions to Burnes, Sept. 5, 1836.

[13] *Ibid.*, Encl. 20, minute on commerce and navigation on the Indus by Auckland, Aug. 29, 1836.

[14] Metcalfe to Auckland, Oct. 15, 1836, *Auckland Papers*, No. 37689.

[15] PGR, 107/8, Macnaghten to Wade, Aug. 2, 1836, NAI, Foreign Department, *Secret Dispatch to the Secret Committee*, No. 4, Nov. 28, 1836.

[16] *Ibid.*, 107/16, Macnaghten to Wade, Sept. 27, 1836.

[17] IOR, *Indian Secret Letters*, Nov. 28, 1836.

[18] *Ibid.*

[19] *Ibid.*, Encl., Macnaghten to Wade, Sept. 26, 1836.

[20] *Ibid.*

[21] IOR, *Board's Secret Drafts*, March 7, 1835.

[22] *Ibid.*

[23] PGR, 142/70, Wade to Government, Oct. 5, 1836.

129

NOTES

[24] Macnaghten to Wade, Nov. 14, 1836, quoted by P. N. Khera, *British Policy Toward Sindh up to the Annexation*, p. 35 n.

[25] *Ibid.*, p. 35.

[26] PGR, 107/30, Macnaghten to Wade, Nov. 7, 1836.

[27] J. D. Cunningham, *History of the Sikhs*, p. 205.

[28] IOR, *Indian Secret Letters*, Jan. 2, 1837.

[29] *Ibid.*, Jan. 2, 1837, Encl. 2, Pottinger to Government, Nov. 30, 1836.

[30] *Ibid.*, No. 3, April 10, 1837, Encl. 41A, Wade to Government, March 13, 1837.

[31] *Ibid.*, No. 3, April 10, 1837.

[32] *Ibid.*, Encl. 33, Pottinger to Macnaghten, Oct. 12, 1836.

[33] *Ibid.*, No. 22, Dec. 27, 1837, Encl. 3, Pottinger to Macnaghten, June 3, 1837.

[34] *Ibid.*, No. 9, Aug. 5, 1837.

[35] *Ibid.*

[36] *Ibid.*, Encl. 9, Macnaghten to Pottinger, May 1, 1837.

[37] *Ibid.*, No. 9, Aug. 5, 1837, paragraph 29.

[38] *Ibid.*, No. 15, Oct. 9, 1837, Encl. 91, Pottinger to Macnaghten, May 11, 1837.

[39] *Ibid.*, Encl. 93, Macnaghten to Pottinger, June 19, 1837.

[40] *Ibid.*, Encl. 91, Pottinger to Macnaghten, May 11, 1837.

[41] *Ibid.*

[42] *Ibid.*, Encl. 93, Macnaghten to Pottinger, June 19, 1837.

[43] *Ibid.*, No. 22, Dec. 27, 1837, Encl. 3, Pottinger to Macnaghten, June 3, 1837.

[44] *Ibid.*, No. 22, Dec. 27, 1837.

[45] *Ibid.*, Encl. 18, Macnaghten to Captain C. M. Wade, Sept. 25, 1837.

[46] *Ibid.*, Encl. 19, Macnaghten to Pottinger, Sept. 25, 1837. Also PGR 119/58, Macnaghten to Pottinger, Sept. 25, 1837.

[47] *Ibid.*, No. 4, Feb. 21, 1838.

[48] *Ibid.*, No. 6, April 23, 1838. For text of treaty see Aitchison, *A Collection of Treaties, Engagements and Sanads*, VIII, 328.

NOTES TO CHAPTER 4
(Pp. 43–67)

[1] IOR, *Indian Secret Letters*, No. 3, April 10, 1837, Encl. 58, Macnaghten to McNeil, April 10, 1837.

NOTES

[2] *Ibid.*, No. 15, Oct. 9, 1837, Encl. 9, Wade to Macnaghten, Aug. 25, 1837.

[3] *Ibid.*, Encl. 11, Minute by the Governor-General, Sept. 7, 1837.

[4] *Ibid.*, No. 4, Feb. 21, 1838.

[5] *Ibid.*, No. 18, Aug. 13, 1838.

[6] PGR, 108/68, Burnes to Macnaghten, December 30, 1837.

[7] IOR, *Indian Secret Letters*, No. 18, Aug. 13, 1838.

[8] IOR, *Board's Secret Drafts*, Dec. 4, 1838.

[9] IOR, *Indian Secret Letters*, March 5, 1835.

[10] *Ibid.*, Nov. 28, 1836.

[11] C. U. Aitchison, *A Collection of Treaties, Engagements and Sanads*, Vol. I (Punjab), No. 6.

[12] IOR, *Indian Secret Letters*, No. 18, Aug. 13, 1838.

[13] *Ibid.*

[14] *Ibid.*, Sept. 24, 1838, Encl. 83, Pottinger to Macnaghten, August 13, 1838.

[15] Auckland to Lushington, Sept. 17, 1838, *Auckland Papers*, No. 37694.

[16] *Ibid.*, Auckland to Hobhouse, May 2, 1839, No. 37695.

[17] IOR, *Indian Secret Letters*, Sept. 24, 1838, Encl. No. 84, Macnaghten to Pottinger, Sept. 6, 1838.

[18] *Ibid.*

[19] *Ibid.*, No. 31, Dec. 31, 1838, Encl. 3, Macnaghten to Pottinger (no date).

[20] *Ibid.*

[21] *Ibid.*, Encl. 5, Macnaghten to Pottinger, Nov. 19, 1838. Auckland also mentioned that the British might find it useful to support the pretensions of a Kalhora descendant at Bekanir who had made overtures to the British. IOR, *Indian Secret Letters*, No. 31, Dec. 31, 1838, Encl. 3, Macnaghten to Pottinger (no date).

[22] Aitchison, *op. cit.*, VIII, 295–296.

[23] IOR, *Indian Secret Letters*, No. 31, Dec. 31, 1838, Encl. No. 5, Macnaghten to Pottinger, Nov. 19, 1838.

[24] *Ibid.*, Encl. No. 7, Macnaghten to Pottinger, Dec. 13, 1838.

[25] *Ibid.*, March 13, 1839, Encl. Pottinger to Eastwick, Jan. 13, 1839.

[26] *Ibid.*

[27] *Ibid.*

[28] SC, No. 130, Eastwick to Pottinger, Jan. 26, 1839.

[29] *Ibid.*

[30] *Ibid.*

[31] *Ibid.*

131

NOTES

[32] *Ibid.*

[33] IOR, *Indian Secret Letters*, No. 32, Sept. 19, 1839, Encl. 4, Pottinger to Maddock, July 6, 1839. For a highly inaccurate description of the capture of Karachi by a participant, see M. B. Neill, *Recollections of Four Years Service in the East with His Majesty's Fortieth Regiment.*

[34] *Ibid.*

[35] *Ibid.*

[36] *Ibid.*, No. 32, Sept. 19, 1839, Encl. 6, Pottinger to Maddock, July 30, 1839.

[37] *Ibid.*

[38] *Ibid.*, No. 4, March 13, 1839 and No. 32, Sept. 19, 1839.

[39] *Ibid.*, Encl., Maddock to Pottinger, Sept. 2, 1839.

[40] *Ibid.*, No. 18, Aug. 13, 1838.

[41] Aitchison, *op. cit.*, VIII, 335–338.

[42] *Ibid.*, pp. 332–333.

[43] SC, No. 108, Burnes to Secretary with the Governor-General, Dec. 28, 1838.

[44] *Ibid.*

[45] Aitchison, *op. cit.*, VIII, 328–330.

[46] *Ibid.*

[47] *Ibid.*, pp. 331–332.

[48] IOR, *Indian Secret Letters*, No. 4, March 13, 1839.

[49] Aitchison, *op. cit.*, VIII, 336–338.

[50] IOR, *Indian Secret Letters*, No. 4, March 13, 1839.

[51] *Ibid.*, marginal notation.

[52] IOR, *Board's Secret Drafts*, No. 4, July 8, 1839.

[53] IOR, *Indian Secret Letters*, No. 7, Feb. 5, 1840, Encl. 453, Maddock to Bell, Sept. 5, 1839.

[54] *Ibid.*, No. 141, Dec. 20, 1840, Encl. 7, Maddock to Nott, Dec. 7, 1840.

[55] Hobhouse to Carnac, April 5, 1841, *Hobhouse Papers.*

[56] IOR, *Board's Secret Drafts*, March 31, 1841.

[57] Auckland to Broughton, June 9, 1841, *Broughton Papers*, No. 36474.

[58] IOR, *Indian Secret Letters*, No. 64, Aug. 20, 1841, Encl. 27, Maddock to Outram, July 26, 1841.

[59] Outram was to be assigned five first-class assistants, five second-class assistants, and four third-class assistants.

[60] Auckland to Sir Richard Jenkins, May 21, 1839, *Auckland Papers*, No. 37696.

[61] *Ibid.*, Auckland to Hobhouse, May 10, 1839.

NOTES

[62] *Ibid.*, Auckland to Bell, May 18, 1839.

[63] Auckland to Hobhouse, Sept. 25, 1839, *Broughton Papers*, No. 36474.

[64] Report on the Indus steamer by Commander Carless, June 22, 1840, No. 38, *Broughton Papers*, No. 36471. Three steamers were shipped to the Indus for purposes of its navigation—the *Meteor*, the *Planet*, and the *Indus*.

[65] Auckland to Carnac, June 27, 1840, *Auckland Papers*, No. 37700.

[66] *Ibid.*, Auckland to Hobhouse, July 10, 1840.

[67] IOR, *Indian Secret Letters*, No. 57, June 6, 1841, Encl. 3, Outram to Maddock, April 6, 1840.

[68] *Ibid.*

[69] *Ibid.*, Encl. 4, Maddock to Outram, May 11, 1840.

[70] *Ibid.*, No. 29, April 14, 1840, Encl. 53/54, Pottinger to Outram, Jan 25, 1840.

[71] IOR, *Bengal Secret and Political Consultations*, March 5, 1833, Bentinck to Pottinger, Oct. 10, 1833.

[72] Article 11: "No toll will be levied on trading boats passing up and down the river Indus, from the sea to the northern most point of that stream within the territories of the Ameers of Hyderabad."

[73] IOR, *Indian Secret Letters*, No. 71, July 6, 1840, Encl. 11, Outram to Maddock, May 11, 1840.

[74] Jeth Anund was subsequently discharged and his office abolished at Outram's request.

[75] IOR, *Indian Secret Letters*, No. 71, July 6, 1840, Encl. 11, Outram to Maddock, May 11, 1840.

[76] *Ibid.*

[77] *Ibid.*

[78] *Ibid.*, H. Torrens to Outram, June 22, 1840.

[79] *Ibid.*

[80] *Ibid.*

[81] Auckland to Peel, Feb. 28, 1841, *Auckland Papers*, No. 37703.

[82] IOR, *Indian Secret Letters*, No. 32, April 22, 1841, Encl. 23, Maddock to Outram, April 5, 1841.

[83] *Ibid.*

[84] *Ibid.*, No. 64, Aug. 20, 1841, Encl. 28, Bell to Maddock, May 28, 1841.

[85] *Ibid.*, Encl. 29, Outram to Maddock, May 22, 1841.

[86] *Ibid.*

[87] *Ibid.*, Encl. 10, Maddock to Outram, July 5, 1841.

[88] *Ibid.*, No. 87, Oct. 21, 1841.

NOTES

[89] SC, No. 319, Leckie to Outram, Feb. 6, 1842.

[90] *Ibid.* The article stated that the two parties to the treaty were not to covet each other's possessions.

[91] *Ibid.*

[92] IOR, *Indian Secret Letters*, No. 7, Jan. 22, 1842, Encl. 20, Outram to Maddock, Nov. 26, 1841.

[93] *Ibid.*, Encl. 21, Maddock to Outram, Dec. 20, 1841.

[94] Outram was able to gain their expulsion when a member of the family was discovered to have forged Outram's seal to aid him in the acquisition of a *jagir*, for a friend, from Sher Mahomed of Mirpur. SC, No. 281, Outram to Government Secretary, Jan. 11, 1841.

NOTES TO CHAPTER 5
(Pp. 68–89)

[1] Palmerston to Hobhouse, Oct. 24, 1838. *Hobhouse Papers*, Vol. 838, p. 482.

[2] IOR, *Indian Secret Letters*, No. 5, April 30, 1842.

[3] *Ibid.*, Encl. 3. Governor-General to the political agents deputed to native courts, April 22, 1842.

[4] Sir Algernon Law, *India Under Lord Ellenborough*, p. 28. Memorandum by the Governor-General on Indian foreign policy, April 27, 1842.

[5] IOR, *Board's Secret Drafts*, No. 903, Dec. 3, 1843.

[6] Ellenborough to Fitzgerald, Oct. 18, 1843, *Ellenborough Papers*, No. 77.

[7] The result of an indiscreet speech.

[8] Edward Law, *A Political Diary 1828–1830*, I, 127–131.

[9] *Ibid.*, II, 176.

[10] William Napier, *Life and Opinions of Sir Charles Napier*, III, 28.

[11] See John Mawson, *Records of the Indian Command of General Sir Charles Napier.*

[12] A young subaltern once remarked: "When I see the old man incessantly on his horse, how can I be idle when I am young and strong? By God, I would go into a loaded cannon's mouth if he ordered me." Quoted by T. Rice Holmes, *Sir Charles Napier*, p. 51.

[13] William Napier, *op. cit.*, III, 332.

NOTES

[14] *Ibid.,* 184.

[15] *Ibid.,* 28.

[16] *Ibid.,* II, 189.

[17] *Ibid.,* 266.

[18] Quoted in H. T. Lambrick, *Sir Charles Napier and Sind,* p. 36.

[19] IOR, *Indian Secret Letters,* No. 114, Oct. 19, 1840; No. 125, November 16, 1840.

[20] *Ibid.,* No. 25, March 22, 1842, Encl. 68, Outram to Maddock, Feb. 21, 1842.

[21] *Ibid.,* No. 62, Dec. 20, 1842, Encl. 68, Clerk to Maddock, Nov. 12, 1842.

[22] *Ibid.,* No. 52, Nov. 19, 1842, Encl. 115, Outram to Napier, Oct. 17, 1842.

[23] *Ibid.,* No. 62, Dec. 20, 1842, Encl. 68, Clerk to Maddock, Nov. 12, 1842.

[24] *Ibid.,* No. 52, Nov. 19, 1842, Encl., Meer Nusseer Khan of Hyderabad to Beebruck Boogtie, no date.

[25] SC, No. 350, Maddock to Outram, July 10, 1842.

[26] *Ibid.,* No. 339, Maddock to Outram, June 4, 1842.

[27] *Ibid.,* No. 347, Outram to Maddock, June 26, 1842.

[28] Napier, *op. cit.,* II, 196.

[29] IOR, *Indian Secret Letters,* No. 49, Oct. 19, 1842, Encl. 58, Napier to Maddock, Oct. 5, 1842.

[30] SC, No. 357, Nasir Khan to Jeyt Mull, Aug. 19, 1842.

[31] IOR, *Indian Secret Letters,* No. 49, Oct. 19, 1842, Encl. 58, Napier to Maddock, Oct. 5, 1842.

[32] SC, No. 364, Maddock to Napier, Sept. 11, 1842.

[33] IOR, *Indian Secret Letters,* No. 52, Nov. 19, 1842, Encl. 117, Ellenborough to Napier, Nov. 4, 1842.

[34] SC, No. 363, Ellenborough to Outram, Sept. 11, 1842.

[35] SC, No. 364, Maddock to Napier, Sept. 11, 1842.

[36] IOR, *Indian Secret Letters,* No. 49, Oct. 19, 1842, Encl. 60, Maddock to Napier, Oct. 14, 1842.

[37] SC, No. 379, Encl. 3, Outram to Napier, Oct. 14, 1842.

[38] *Ibid.,* Encl. 3, Outram to Napier, Oct. 14, 1842. In SC, No. 378, Oct. 25, 1842, Ellenborough wrote to Napier deprecating the idea of assuming control of Shikarpur as he thought the possession of Sukkur would be preferable due to its favorable position for attracting trade.

[39] SC, No. 379, Encl. 1, observations by Sir Charles Napier on the occupation of Sind, Oct. 17, 1842.

[40] *Ibid.*

NOTES

[41] IOR, *Indian Secret Letters*, No. 49, Oct. 19, 1843, Encl. 109, Ellenborough to Napier, Oct. 23, 1842.

[42] *Ibid.*, No. 62, Dec. 20, 1842, Encl. 64, Ellenborough to Napier, Nov. 24, 1842.

[43] *Ibid.*, Encl. 81, Napier to Ellenborough, Nov. 30, 1842.

[44] *Ibid.*, No. 49, Oct. 19, 1842, Encl. 61, general order by the Governor-General, Oct. 19, 1842.

[45] Napier, *op. cit.*, II, 218.

[46] Lambrick, *op. cit.*, p. 47.

[47] E. B. Eastwick, *Dry Leaves from Young Egypt*, p. 116.

[48] Lord Colchester, *History of the Indian Administration of Lord Ellenborough*, p. 347.

[49] Napier, *op. cit.*, II, 181.

[50] Colchester, *op. cit.*, p. 347.

[51] Ellenborough to Arthur, Nov. 17, 1842, *Ellenborough Papers*, No. 76.

[52] Napier, *op. cit.*, II, 240.

[53] Napier to Ellenborough, Oct. 17, 1842, *Ellenborough Papers*, No. 62.

[54] IOR, *Indian Secret Letters*, No. 52, Nov. 19, 1842, Encl. 116, Ellenborough to Napier, Nov. 3, 1842; Encl. 117, Ellenborough to Napier, Nov. 4, 1842.

[55] *Ibid.*

[56] *Ibid.*

[57] Lambrick, *op. cit.*, p. 75.

[58] A *serai* is an encampment.

[59] IOR, *Indian Secret Letters*, No. 52, Nov. 19, 1842, Encl. 127, Ellenborough to Napier, Nov. 14, 1842.

[60] C. U. Aitchison, *A Collection to Treaties, Engagements and Sanads*, VIII, 339–343. The provisions of the proposed treaties with the Hyderabad and Khairpur amirs were similar. The amirs were relieved of all tribute payments in return for the cession of Karachi and Tatta by Hyderabad and Sukkur, Bukkur, and Rohri, by Khairpur. In addition, the Khan of Bahawalpur was to acquire Bhung Bhara, Sabzalkot, and all territory between Rohri and Bahawalpur. Other articles provided for the right of the British to cut wood along the banks of the Indus and to control the coinage of Sind.

[61] James Outram, *The Conquest of Scinde: A Commentary*, p. 149.

[62] Lambrick, *op. cit.*, p. 77.

136

NOTES

[63] SC, No. 403, Intelligence from Sinde, Nov. 7–13, 1842.

[64] *Ibid.*, No. 405, Intelligence from Hyderabad, Nov. 10–15, 1842.

[65] *Ibid.*, No. 404, Intelligence from Sukkur, Nov. 12, 1842.

[66] *Ibid.*, Intelligence from Sukkur, Nov. 13, 1842.

[67] *Ibid.*, No. 408, Intelligence from T. Clibborn, Nov. 15–20, 1842.

[68] IOR, *Indian Secret Letters*, No. 62, Dec. 20, 1842, Encl. 74, Napier to Ellenborough, Nov. 23, 1842.

[69] Napier, *op. cit.*, II, 243.

[70] Lambrick, *op. cit.*, p. 86.

[71] IOR, *Indian Secret Letters*, No. 62, Dec. 20, 1842, Encl. 79, Napier to Ellenborough, Nov. 26, 1842.

[72] *Ibid.*

[73] *Ibid.*, Encl. 80, Ellenborough to Napier, Dec. 4, 1842.

[74] SC, No. 421, Napier to the Governor-General, Nov. 30, 1842.

[75] *Ibid.*, No. 431, Intelligence of Dec. 8, 1842.

[76] IOR, *Indian Secret Letters*, No. 62, Dec. 20, 1842, Encl. 83, Napier to Ellenborough, Dec. 7, 1842.

[77] SC, No. 431, Intelligence from T. Clibborn, Dec. 7–13, 1842.

[78] IOR, *Indian Secret Letters*, No. 62, Dec. 20, 1842, Encl. 87, Napier to the Amirs of Khairpur, Dec. 9, 1842.

[79] SC, No. 428, Napier to the Governor-General, Dec. 9, 1842.

[80] Lambrick, *op. cit.*, p. 92.

[81] SSC, No. 8, Sir Charles Napier to Mir Rustam of Khairpur, Dec. 12, 1842.

[82] SC, No. 433, Mir Rustam to Napier, no date.

[83] *Ibid.*, No. 436, Intelligence from Sinde, Dec. 14–19, 1842.

[84] SSC, No. 11, Napier to Rustam, Dec. 18, 1842.

[85] SC, No. 439, Napier to the Governor-General, Dec. 20, 1842.

[86] *Ibid.*, No. 431, Intelligence of Dec. 10, 1842.

[87] Lambrick, *op. cit.*, p. 96.

[88] SSC, No. 10, Napier to Rustam, Dec. 18, 1842.

[89] Napier to Ellenborough, Dec. 20, 1842, *Ellenborough Papers*, No. 62.

[90] Lambrick, *op. cit.*, p. 98. See IOR, *Indian Secret Letters*, No. 39, Sept. 21, 1843, Encl. 67, Napier to Ellenborough, Aug. 16, 1843, for the text of the treaty supposedly written in a Koran on Dec. 20, 1842, under the terms of which Mir Rustam was said to have abdicated the Turban in favor of Ali Murad.

NOTES

⁹¹ IOR, *Indian Secret Letters*, No. 31, Aug. 14, 1843, Napier to Ali Murad, Dec. 23, 1842.

⁹² SC, No. 445, Napier to Ellenborough, Dec. 27, 1842.

⁹³ SSC, No. 15, Proclamation by Sir Charles Napier, Jan. 1, 1843.

⁹⁴ IOR, *Indian Secret Letters*, No. 31, Aug. 14, 1843, Napier to Rustam, Jan. 2, 1843.

NOTES TO CHAPTER 6
(Pp. 90–112)

[1] SC, No. 444, Intelligence from T. Clibborn, Dec. 22, 1842.

[2] *Ibid.*, No. 445, Napier to Ellenborough, Dec. 27, 1842.

[3] *Ibid.*, No. 444, Intelligence from Dec. 21–27, 1842; No. 449, Intelligence from Dec. 29 to Jan. 22, 1843.

[4] *Ibid.*, No. 449, Intelligence for Jan. 4, 1843.

[5] *Ibid.*, Jan. 5, 1842.

[6] *Ibid.*, No. 453, Napier to Ellenborough, Jan. 7, 1843.

[7] H. T. Lambrick, *Sir Charles Napier and Sind*, p. 110.

[8] *Ibid.*

[9] SC, No. 445, Napier to Ellenborough, Dec. 27, 1842.

[10] William Napier, *Life and Opinions of Sir Charles Napier*, II, 289.

[11] IOR, *Indian Secret Letters*, No. 12, Feb. 19, 1843, Encl. 31, Napier to Ellenborough, Jan. 17, 1843.

[12] Lambrick, *op. cit.*, p. 112.

[13] Sir F. Goldsmid, *James Outram*, I, 308.

[14] SC, No. 458, Napier to the amirs of Upper and Lower Sind, Jan. 15, 1843.

[15] SSC, No. 27, Outram to Napier, Jan. 18, 1843.

[16] *Ibid.*, No. 24, Outram to Napier, Jan. 17, 1843.

[17] *Ibid.*, No. 28, Napier to Outram, Jan. 20, 1843.

[18] *Ibid.*, No. 29, Outram to Napier, Jan. 22, 1843.

[19] *Ibid.*

[20] IOR, *Indian Secret Letters*, No. 39, Sept. 21, 1843, Encl., Outram to Napier, Jan. 22, 1843, 9 P.M.

[21] *Ibid.*, No. 44, Sept. 21, 1843, Encl. Napier to Outram, Jan. 23, 1843.

[22] *Ibid.*, No. 39, Sept. 21, 1843, Encl. Outram to Napier, Jan. 24, 1843.

[23] Of this total, Rs. 150,000 annual income had been acquired

NOTES

by Ali Murad through territories ceded to him by his relatives under the provisions of the Treaty of Nunahar which had ended, in Ali Murad's favor, a war between the Khairpur amirs over property rights.

[24] IOR, *Indian Secret Letters*, No. 39, Sept. 21, 1843, Encl. Outram to Napier, Jan. 24, 1843.

[25] *Ibid.*, No. 12, Feb. 19, 1843, Encl. 35, Proclamation by Napier to the amirs of Upper Sind, Jan. 27, 1843.

[26] *Ibid.*, No. 12, Feb. 19, 1843, Encl. 35, Napier to Ellenborough, Jan. 28, 1843.

[27] Napier, *op. cit.*, II, 297–303.

[28] Goldsmid, *op. cit.*, I, 305.

[29] James Outram, *The Conquest of Scinde: A Commentary*, as quoted by Lambrick, *op. cit.*, p. 112.

[30] Arthur to Ellenborough, Aug. 11, 1842, *Ellenborough Papers*, No. 39.

[31] Quoted by Lambrick, *op. cit.*, p. 76.

[32] Napier, *op. cit.*, III, 332.

[33] SSC, No. 36, Napier to Outram, Jan. 28, 1843.

[34] SC, No. 449, Intelligence of Jan. 21–22, 1843.

[35] Lambrick, *op. cit.*, pp. 125–126.

[36] SSC, No. 178, Jan. 22, 1843, evidence given by Peer Budroodeen, former confidential servant of former Amir Sobdar Khan of Hyderabad, no date.

[37] *Ibid.*, No. 45, Napier to Outram, Feb. 4, 1843.

[38] IOR, *Indian Secret Letters*, No. 31, Aug. 14, 1843, Encl., notes of conference of Feb. 8, 1843.

[39] *Ibid.*

[40] *Ibid.*, No. 44, Sept. 21, 1843, Encl., Outram to Napier, Feb. 8, 1843.

[41] *Ibid.*, No. 31, Aug. 14, 1843, Encl., Outram to Napier, Feb. 11, 1843.

[42] *Ibid.*, Encl., Outram to Napier, Feb. 12, 1843, A.M.

[43] *Ibid.*, Encl., Outram to Napier, Feb. 12, 1843, P.M.

[44] *Ibid.*, March 13, 1843, Encl. 3, Napier to Ellenborough, Feb. 13, 1843.

[45] *Ibid.*

[46] *Ibid.*, No. 44, Sept. 21, 1843, Encl. 4, Outram to Napier, Feb. 10, 1843.

[47] *Ibid.*, March 13, 1843, Encl. 3, Napier to Ellenborough, Feb. 13, 1843.

[48] SSC, No. 68, Outram to Napier, Feb. 13, 1843, 12 A.M.

139

NOTES

[49] *Ibid.*, No. 69, Outram to Napier, Feb. 13, 1843, 4:30 P.M.

[50] IOR, *Indian Secret Letters*, No. 44, Sept. 21, 1843, Encl., Outram to Napier, Feb. 11, 1843.

[51] IOR, *Indian Secret Letters*, No. 31, Aug. 14, 1843, Encl., Napier to Outram, Feb. 13, 1843.

[52] *Ibid.*, March 13, 1843, Encl. 3, Napier to Ellenborough, Feb. 13, 1843.

[53] *Ibid.*, Encl., Napier to Outram, Feb. 15, 1843.

[54] SSC, No. 74, Outram to Lieutenant-Colonel Booth, Feb. 14, 1843.

[55] *Ibid.*, Outram to Lieutenant-Colonel Boileau, Feb. 14, 1843.

[56] *Ibid.*, No. 77, Outram to Mir Shahdad, Feb. 14, 1843.

[57] *Ibid.*, No. 75, Outram to the Hyderabad amirs, Feb. 14, 1843.

[58] E. B. Eastwick, *Dry Leaves from Young Egypt*, p. 201.

[59] Outram, *op. cit.*, p. 423.

[60] Lambrick, *op. cit.*, p. 133.

[61] Goldsmid, *op. cit.*, I, 320–323.

[62] For an excellent discussion of the war in Sind, see Lambrick, *op. cit.*, chapter iii.

[63] As was pointed out previously, the famous "Peccavi" story is apocryphal.

[64] T. R. Holmes, *Sir Charles Napier*, p. 80.

[65] IOR, *Indian Secret Letters*, No. 31, Aug. 14, 1843, Encl. 76, Napier to Ellenborough, July 11, 1843.

[66] SSC, No. 57, Napier to Outram, Feb. 11, 1843.

[67] IOR, *Indian Secret Letters*, No. 48, June 13, 1843.

[68] *Ibid.*, No. 23, July 20, 1843, Encl., Ellenborough to Napier, July 20, 1843.

[69] *Ibid.*, No. 31, Aug. 14, 1843, Encl. 76, Napier to Ellenborough, July 11, 1843.

[70] SC, No. 473, Napier to the Governor-General, Feb. 10, 1843.

[71] IOR, *Indian Secret Letters*, No. 22, July 19, 1843.

[72] Fitzgerald to Ellenborough, Feb. 5, 1843, *Ellenborough Papers*, No. 42.

[73] Ripon to Ellenborough, June 3, 1843, *Ripon Papers*, No. 40865.

[74] IOR, *Indian Secret Letters*, March 13, 1843.

[75] Peel to Ripon, Dec. 9, 1843, *Ripon Papers*, No. 40866.

[76] Algernon Law, *India Under Lord Ellenborough*, p. 43.

[77] Peel to Ripon, Dec. 9, 1843, *Ripon Papers*, No. 40866.

[78] IOR, *Indian Secret Letters*, March 13, 1843, Encl. 40, General orders by the Governor-General, March 13, 1843.

NOTES

[79] *Ibid.*, No. 31, Aug. 14, 1843, Encl., Proclamation by Napier, March 5, 1843.

[80] *Ibid.*, No. 30, April 22, 1843.

[81] Napier, *op. cit.*, III, 349.

[82] Hansard, *Parliamentary Debates*, third series, XCIV, July 20, 1847.

[83] Ripon to Ellenborough, July 6, 1843, *Ripon Papers*, No. 40865.

[84] *Ibid.*, Ripon to Ellenborough, Dec. 4, 1843, No. 40865.

[85] IOR, *Indian Secret Letters*, No. 33, Aug. 28, 1843.

[86] *Ibid.*

[87] Lambrick, *op. cit.*, p. 250.

[88] It was not unusual in the first half of the nineteenth century for members of Parliament to vote against their party, as party lines were not yet rigidly drawn.

[89] Palmerston was much amused to see Ellenborough, the critic of the Afghan policy, "turned conqueror." Palmerston to Hobhouse, April 10, 1842, *Broughton Papers*, No. 46915.

[90] Hansard, *Parliamentary Debates*, third series, LXXII, Feb. 8, 1844.

[91] Peel to Ripon, Aug. 17, 1843, *Ripon Papers*, No. 40865.

[92] Hansard, *Parliamentary Debates*, third series, LXXII, Feb. 8, 1844. For a full report of the debate see Lambrick, *op. cit.*, pp. 243–247.

[93] *Ibid.*

[94] Two blue books were printed by the Government on the subject of the annexation of Sind and although the material was quite voluminous, some documents which were evidently considered embarrasing were not included in the collections.

[95] East India Company, *Debates in East India House*, Nov. 17, 1843.

[96] *General Court Minutes*, 1799–1844, VI, Jan. 26, 1844.

[97] Ellenborough was destined to become Chairman of the Board of Control again after his recall.

[98] *Parliamentary Papers*, 1852–3, LXVII, Series D, No. 11, as quoted by Lambrick, *op. cit.*, p. 272.

[99] Lambrick, *op. cit.*, pp. 271–272, 349, 353–355.

[100] *Parliamentary Papers*, 1852–3, LXVII, Series D, No. 12, as quoted by Lambrick, *op. cit.*, p. 355.

[101] Jacob to Outram, May 28, 1850, as quoted in Lambrick, *op. cit.*, p. 355.

[102] Lambrick, *op. cit.*, pp. 353–355.

NOTES

[103] Many members of the Talpur family until recently held positions of prominence in West Pakistan.

NOTES TO CHAPTER 7
(Pp. 113–120)

[1] IOR, *Indian Secret Letters*, July 2, 1832, Encl. 24, Pottinger to Prinsep, April 14, 1832.

[2] *Ibid.*, No. 5, April 30, 1842, Encl. 3, Governor-General to the political agents, April 26, 1842.

[3] Auckland to Hobhouse, March 21, 1841, *Auckland Papers*, No. 37704.

[4] Lord Colchester, *History of the Indian Administration of Lord Ellenborough*, pp. 356–357.

[5] Arthur to Ellenborough, Feb. 26, 1843, *Ellenborough Papers*, No. 41.

[6] Hansard, *Parliamentary Debates*, third series, LXXII, Feb. 8, 1844.

[7] IOR, *Indian Secret Letters*, No. 33, Aug. 28, 1843.

[8] Pottinger described the annexation in the *Morning Chronicle* as "the most unprincipled and disgraceful act that ever stained the annals of our empire in India." Quoted by H. T. Lambrick, *Sir Charles Napier and Sind*, p. 243.

[9] Outram asked George Clerk, the British envoy at Lahore, to induce Sher Singh to answer the letter from Rustam in such a way as to elicit a more definite reply than the ambiguous original. Outram intended to intercept this answer, and he wrote Clerk: "I should not be sorry to afford Government grounds for making an example." (SC, No. 338, Outram to Clerk, May 1, 1842.)

[10] A. P. Thornton, *The Imperial Idea and Its Enemies*, pp. 68–69.

[11] Jawaharlal Nehru, *Toward Freedom*, pp. 271–272.

[12] Quoted by C. E. Carrington, *The British Overseas*, p. 430.

[13] BGR, *Secret and Political Department Diaries*, No. 133, p. 7741, Crow's account of Sind.

[14] Charles Masson, *Narrative of Various Journeys in Balochistan, Afghanistan, the Panjab and Kalat*, II, 131, 465, 467.

[15] Lambrick, *op. cit.*, pp. 14–29.

[16] G. C. Lewis, *Letters of the Rt. Hon. Sir George Cornewall Lewis bart., to Various Friends*, p. 90.

142

Bibliography

MANUSCRIPT SOURCES

British Museum, London
    Auckland Papers, 1836–1841.
    Hobhouse (Lord Broughton) Papers and Diaries, 1837–1844.
    Napier Papers, 1818–1844.
    Peel Papers, 1843–1844.
    Ripon Papers, 1843–1844.
Bombay Government Records, Bombay
    Political Diaries, 1809–1821.
    Secret and Political Diaries, 1799–1844.
    Secret Diaries, 1810–1816.
India Office Library, London
    Bengal Secret Proceedings, 1820–1826.
    Bengal Secret and Political Consultations, 1820–1830.
    Bengal Secret and Separate Consultations, 1808–1834.
    Bengal Secret and Separate Proceedings, 1808–1834.
    Bengal Secret Letters and Enclosures, 1808–1832.
    Board's Collections, 1799–1844.
    Board's Drafts of Secret Letters to India, 1799–1844.
    Board of Control Letter Books.
    Bombay Secret Proceedings, 1820–1826.
    General Court Minutes: Resolutions and Motions of the Court, 1799–1844
    Hobhouse (Lord Broughton) Papers, 1836–1841.
    Home and Miscellaneous Series, 1798–1809.
    Indian Political and Foreign Consultations, 1806–1808.
    Indian Political Consultations, 1806–1808.
    Indian Secret Consultations, 1837.
    Indian Secret Letters to England and Enclosures, 1832–1844.
    Indian Secret Proceedings, 1830–1838.
    Letters from the Board of Control to the East India Company, 1829–1844.
    Letters from the East India Company to the Board of Control, 1843–1844.
    Selections from the Pre-Mutiny Records of the Commissioner in Sind, 1830–1844.
National Archives of India, New Delhi
    Indian Political Consultations, 1812–1845.
    Indian Political Dispatches to the Court of Directors, 1799–1844.

145

BIBLIOGRAPHY

Indian Political Proceedings, 1812–1845.
Indian Secret Consultations, 1812–1845.
Indian Secret Dispatches to the Secret Committee, 1799–1844.
Indian Secret Proceedings, 1812–1845.

Public Record Office, London
Ellenborough Papers, 1829–1844.

Punjab Government Records, Lahore, West Pakistan.
Ludhiana Agency Records, 1829–1841.

University of Nottingham, Library, Nottingham, England.
Bentinck Papers, 1829–1835.

OFFICIAL AND SEMIOFFICIAL PUBLICATIONS

Aitchison, C. U. *A Collection of Treaties, Engagements and Sanads Relating to India and Neighboring Countries*, Calcutta: Government of India Publications Branch, 1932, 12 vols.

Great Britain, Parliament. *Copies of the Acts of the Government of India*, 1834–1838. London: 1840.

———— *Correspondence Relative to Sind*, 1838–1843. London: T. R. Harrison, 1843.

———— *Correspondence Relative to Sinde, Supplementary to the Papers Presented to Parliament in 1843*. London: T. R. Harrison, 1844.

———— *Frontier and Overseas Expeditions from India*. London: Government Printing Office, 1910.

———— *Parliamentary Papers*, 1852–3, LXXVII, Series D.

———— *Papers Relating to Military Operations in Afghanistan*. London: 1843.

———— *Secret Committee on Indian Territories*. 5th Report. London: 1853.

East India Company. *Debates at East India House*, 1799–1844. London: India Office Library.

Hansard. *Parliamentary Debates*. Third series, LXXII (Feb. 8, 1844), LXXX (May 21, 1845), LXXVII (July 16, 1845), XCIV (July 20, 1847).

Hughes, A. W. *A Gazetteer of the Province of Sind*. London: Bell, 1876.

146

BIBLIOGRAPHY

Imperial Gazetteer of India. Vol. II. Oxford: Clarendon Press, 1828.
Imperial Gazetteer of India. Vol. XXII. Oxford: Clarendon Press, 1908.

UNPUBLISHED THESES

Advani, A. B. "The Annexation of Sind." Unpublished Ph.D. thesis, Bombay University, 1928.

Chisti, R. A. "The Conquest of Sind." Unpublished M.A. thesis, School of Oriental and African Studies, University of London, 1938.

Debara, A. K. "James Outram, Political Agent of Sind." Unpublished M.A. thesis, St. Xavier's College, Bombay University, 1943.

Garrett, K. "Lord Ellenborough's Ideas on Indian Policy." Unpublished M.A. thesis, School of Oriental and African Studies, University of London, 1935.

Pandey, K. C. "The Internal Policy of Lord Bentinck." Unpublished Ph.D. thesis, School of Oriental and African Studies, University of London, 1957.

REFERENCE WORKS

Billomoria, N. A. *Bibliography of Publications on Sind and Baluchistan.* London: India Office, 1930.

Bombay Presidency. Sind Commission. *A Handbook of the Government Records Lying in the Office of the Commissioner in Sind.* Karachi: Commissioner's Printing Press, 1933.

———— *Alphabetical Catalogue of the Contents of the Pre-Mutiny Records of the Commissioner in Sind, 1857.* Karachi: Commissioner's Press, 1931.

Foster, W. *Guide to the India Office Records, 1600–1858.* London: India Office Library, 1928.

Kaye, G. R. *European Manuscripts in the India Office Library.* London: H. M. S. O., 1937.

147

BIBLIOGRAPHY

BOOKS

Abbot, J. *Sind: A Restatement*. Bombay: Oxford University Press, 1924.

Allen, Rev. I. N. *Diary of a March Through Scinde and Afghanistan*. London: Hatchard, 1843.

Aspinall, A. *Three Early Nineteenth Century Diaries*. London: Williams and Nogarte, 1952.

Blandenburg, Major Ross of. *The Marquess of Hastings, K. G.* Oxford: Clarendon Press, 1897.

Boulger, D. C. *Lord William Bentinck*. Oxford: Clarendon Press, 1897.

Bruce, William Napier. *Life of General Sir Charles Napier*. London: Murray, 1885.

Buist, George. *Corrections of a Few of the Errors Contained in William Napier's Life of His Brother, Sir Charles Napier, in so far as They Affect the Press of India, in a Letter Addressed to the Author*. London: Smith Elder, 1857.

Burnes Alexander. *Travels into Bokhara*. London: Murray, 1834.

—— *A Voyage on the Indus*. London: Murray, 1834.

Burnes, James. *A Narrative of a Visit to the Court of Sinde*. Edinburgh: Stark, 1831.

Burton, Richard F. *Scinde or the Unhappy Valley*. London: Bentley, 1851. 2 vols.

—— *Sind Revisited*. London: Bentley, 1877.

—— *Scinde and the Races that Inhabit the Valley of the Indus*. London: Allen, 1851.

Brydges, Sir Harford Jones. *The Ameers of Scinde: A Letter to the Hon. Court of Directors of the East India Company*. London: Private Printing, 1843.

Butler, Sir William F. *Sir Charpes Napier*. London: Macmillan, 1890.

Carrington, C. E. *The British Overseas*. Cambridge: University Press, 1950.

Chablani, S. P. *Economic Conditions in Sind, 1592–1843*. Bombay: Orient Longmans, 1951.

Colchester, Lord, *History of the Indian Administration of Lord Ellenborough*. London: Bentley, 1874.

Collection of Pamphlets on India (binder's title). University of California, Los Angeles, library.

148

BIBLIOGRAPHY

Cunningham, J. D. *History of the Sikhs.* Calcutta: Bangasi Press, 1904.

Dennie, William H. *Personal Narrative of the Campaigns in Afghanistan, Sinde and Beloochistan.* Dublin: Curry, 1843.

Dodwell, H. H., and Others. *The Cambridge History of the British Empire.* Cambridge: University Press, 1929. Vol. IV.

Dutt, Romesh. *Economic History of India (The Victorian Age).* London: Kegan, 1903. Vol. II.

Eastwick, E. B. *Dry Leaves from Young Egypt.* London: Madden, 1844.

Eastwick, W. J. *Speeches of Captain Eastwick on the Sinde Question, 16 January, 1844.* London: Smith Elder, 1863.

Elliot, Gilbert. *Life and Letters of the Earl of Minto, 1751–1806.* Ed. by the Countess of Minto. London: Longmans, 1874.

——— *Life and Letters of Gilbert Elliot, First Earl of Minto, from 1807–1814, while Governor-General of India.* Ed. by the Countess of Minto. London: Longmans, 1880.

Evans, Lieutenant-Colonel De Lacey. *On the Designs of Russia.* London: Murray, 1828.

Forbes, A. *The Afghan Wars, 1838–1843, 1878–1880.* London: Seeley, 1906.

Fredunbeg, Mirza Kalichbeg. *The Chachanamah: An Ancient History of Sind,* in two parts. Karachi: Commissioner's Press, 1900.

Goldsmith, Major-General Sir F. J. *James Outram.* London: Smith Elder, 1881. 2 vols.

Green, E. *Compilation of the General Orders and Commands, issued in 1842–47 by Sir C. Napier to the army under his command.* Bombay; Times Press, 1850.

Hardinge, Viscount. *Viscount Hardinge.* Oxford: Clarendon Press, 1897.

Hall, Henry. *The Colonial Office.* London: Longmans, Green, 1937.

Hastings, Marquess of. *The Private Journal of the Marquess of Hastings, K. G., Governor-General and Commander-in-Chief of India.* Ed. by the Marchioness of Bute. London: Saunders and Otley, 1858. 2 vols.

Hobhouse, J. (Lord Broughton). *Recollections of a Long Life,* with additional extracts from his private diary. Ed. by Lady Dorchester. London: Murray, 1909–1911. 6 vols.

Holmes, T. R. *Sir Charles Napier.* Cambridge: University Press, 1925.

Hotchand, Seth Naomul. *Memoires.* Ed. by H. E. M. James, Exeter: Pollard, 1915.

149

BIBLIOGRAPHY

Imlah, Albert H. *Lord Ellenborough.* Cambridge: Harvard University Press, 1939.

Jacob, John. *Memoir of the First Campaign in the Hills North of Cutchee.* London: Allen, 1852.

Jacob, John. *Notes on Sir W. Napier's Administration of Sinde.* Private Printing, no date.

James, Hugo. *A Volunteer's Scramble Through Scinde, the Punjab, Hindostan, and the Himalayah Mountains.* London: Thacker, 1854, 2 vols.

Kaye, J. W. *The Administration of the East India Company.* London: Bentley, 1855.

———— *The Life and Correspondence of Charles, Lord Metcalfe.* London: Smith Elder, 1858. 2 vols.

———— *The Life and Correspondence of Henry St. George Tucker.* London: Bentley, 1854.

———— *The War in Afghanistan.* London: Bentley, 1851. 2 vols.

Keith, A. B. (ed.). *Speeches and Documents on Indian Policy, 1750–1921.* London: Oxford University Press, 1922. Vol. I.

Kennedy, R. H. *Narrative of the Campaign of the Army of the Indus in Sinde and Kabul in 1838–39.* London: Bentley, 1840. 2 vols.

Khera, P. N. *British Policy Toward Sind up to the Annexation.* Lahore: Minerva Book Shop, 1941.

Lal, Mohan. *Life of the Amir Dost Mohammad Khan of Kabul.* London: Longman, 1846. 2 vols.

Lambrick, H. T. *Sir Charles Napier and Sind.* Oxford: Clarendon Press, 1952.

Langley, E. A. *Narrative of a Residence at the Court of Meer Ali Moorad.* London: Hurst and Blackett, 1860. 2 vols.

Law, Edward (Lord Ellenborough). *A Political Diary 1828–1830.* London: Bentley, 1881. 2 vols.

———— *India Under Lord Ellenborough.* Selections from the Ellenborough Papers. Ed. by Sir Algernon Law. London: Murray, 1926.

Lewis, G. C. *Letters of the Rt. Hon. Sir George Cornewall Lewis to Various Friends.* Ed. by G. F. Lewis. London: Longmans, Green, 1870.

Lushington, Henry. *A Great Country's Little Wars.* London: Parker, 1844.

Lutufullah. *Autobiography.* Ed. by E. B. Eastwick. London: Smith Elder, 1863.

150

BIBLIOGRAPHY

Mariwalla, C. L. *Essays on British Policy Towards Sind.* Karachi: Mariwalla, 1946.

Masson, Charles. *Narrative of Various Journeys in Balochistan, Afghanistan, the Panjab and Kalat.* London: Bentley, 1844. 2 vols.

Mawson, John. *Records of the Indian Command of General Sir Charles Napier.* Calcutta: Lepage, 1851.

A *Memoir of the Public Services Rendered by Lieutenant-Colonel Outram.* The University of California, Los Angeles, library copy contains manuscript notations by Outram. London: Smith Elder, 1853.

Misra, B. B. *The Central Administration of the East India Company 1773–1834.* Manchester: Manchester University Press, 1959.

Napier, Charles James. *The Colonies.* London: Boone, 1833.

—— *Colonization, Particularly in Southern Australia with Remarks on Small Farms and Over Population.* London: Boone, 1835.

—— *Defects Civil and Military of the Indian Government.* London: Westerton, 1853.

—— *A Letter to the Right Honorable Sir. J. Hobhouse.* London: Moxon, 1849.

Napier, William. *Comments by Lieutenant-General Sir W. Napier Upon a Memorandum of the Duke of Wellington and other Documents, concerning Lt. Gen. C. J. Napier, with a Defence of Sir C. Napier's Government of Scinde by Captain Rathborne.* London: Westerton, 1854.

—— *The Conquest of Scinde.* London: Boone, 1845.

—— *The History of General Sir Charles Napier's Administration of Scinde.* London: Chapman and Hill, 1851.

—— *The Life and Opinions of Sir Charles Napier.* London: Murray, 1857.

Nehru, J. *Toward Freedom.* Boston: Beacon Press, 1951.

Neil, M. B. *Recollections of Four Years' Service in the East with H. M. Fortieth Regiment.* Comprising an account of the taking of Kurachee in Lower Scinde and operations of the Candahar Division of "the Avenging Army of Afghanistan" in 1841 and 1842; under Major-General Sir W. Nott GCB. London: Bentley, 1845.

Nicholson, A. P. *Scraps of Paper: India's Broken Treaties.* London: Benn, 1930.

Outram, James. *The Conquest of Scinde: A Commentary.* (The University of California, Los Angeles, library copy contains

151

BIBLIOGRAPHY

manuscript notations by Outram.) London: Blackwood, 1846.

—— *A Refutation of Certain Calumnies.* Bombay: Private Printing, 1845.

—— *Rough Notes of the Campaign in Sinde and Afghanistan in 1838–9.* Cornhill: Richardson, 1840.

Pamphlets on Sinde (Eastwick speech, etc.; binder's title.) London: Smith Elder, 1844–45.

Philips, C. H. *The East India Company, 1784–1834.* Manchester: Manchester University Press, 1940.

Pithwalli, M. B. *Sind's Changing Map.* Karachi: Union Press, 1938.

Postans, T. *Personal Observations on Sindh.* London: Longmans, 1843.

Pottinger, Lieutenant Henry. *Travels in Baloochistan and Scinde.* London: Longmans, 1816.

Prinsep, H. T. *History of the Political and Military Transactions in India during the Administration of the Marquess of Hastings.* London: Kingsbury, 1825. 2 vols.

Richardson, E., and A. T. Ritchie. *Lord Auckland and the British Advance Eastward to Burma.* Oxford: Clarendon Press, 1909.

Roberts, P. E. *The History of British India.* London: Oxford University Press, 1952.

Ross, David. *Land of the Five Rivers and Sindh.* London: Chapman and Hall, 1883.

The Scinde Policy: A Few Commentaries on Major-General W. F. P. Napier's Defense of Lord Ellenborough's Government. London: Longmans, 1845.

Sethi, R. R. *The Lahore Darbar,* in the light of the correspondence of Sir C. B. Wade, 1823–1840. Lahore: Punjab Government Record Office Publication, 1950.

Stocqueler, J. H. *Memorials of Afghanistan Illustrative of the British Expedition to and Occupation of Afghanistan and Scinde between the Years 1838–1842.* Calcutta: Ostell and Lepage, 1843.

Taylor, P. M. *Letters from Captain Phillip Taylor to Henry Reeve.* Edited by Sir Patrick Cadell. Oxford: University Press, 1947.

Taylor, P. M. *The Story of My Life.* London: Blackwood, 1877. 2 vols.

Thomas, R. H. *Memoirs on Shikarpoor.* Bombay: Bombay Presidency Press, 1855.

Thompson, E. J. *The Life of Charles, Lord Metcalfe.* London: Faber, 1937.

BIBLIOGRAPHY

Thornton, A. P. *The Imperial Idea and Its Enemies*. London: Macmillan, 1959.

Thornton, Edward. *The History of the British Empire in India*. London: Allen, 1843. Vol. VI.

Trotter, Captain L. J. *The Earl of Auckland*. Oxford: Clarendon Press, 1893.

Tucker, Henry St. George. *Memorials of Indian Government*. London: Bentley, 1853.

Wilson, H. M., and J. S. Mill. *The History of British India 1800–1835*. London: Madden, 1848. 3 vols.

Wilton, J. H. *Scenes in a Soldier's Life*. Montreal: Chalmers, 1848. 2 vols.

Woodruff, Philip. *The Men Who Ruled India: The Founders*. London: Cape, 1953.

Young, Colonel Keith. *Scinde in the Forties*. Ed. by A. F. Scott. London: Constable, 1854.

ARTICLES

Bearce, G. D., Jr. "Lord William Bentinck: The Application of Liberalism in India," *Journal of Modern History*, XXVIII:3 (Sept., 1956), 234–246.

Billimoria, N. D. "The Somra and Summa Dynasties in Sind," *Journal of the Sind Historical Society*, I:2 (Oct., 1942), 77–78.

Burnes, A. "On Sind," *Journal of the Royal Geographical Society*, VII (1838), 11.

Carless, T. G. "Memoir to Accompany the Survey of the Delta of the Indus in 1837," *Journal of the Royal Geographic Society*, VII (1837), 328.

Mariwalla, C. L. "British Adventure in Sind," *Journal of the Sind Historical Society*, VI:1 (June, 1942), 24–42.

Mirchandani, B. D. "Crow's Account of Sind," *Journal of the Sind Historical Society*, I:2 (Oct., 1934).

Schneidman, J. L. "The Proposed Invasion of India by Russia and France in 1801," *Journal of Indian History*, XXV (Aug., 1957), 167–175.

BIBLIOGRAPHY

PERIODICALS AND NEWSPAPERS

Economist, 1843–1845.
Edinburgh *Review*, 1843–1845.
London *Times*, 1799–1845.
Punch, 1843–1845.

Index

Index

Abad, 82
Abdul Nabi, Mian, 2, 9, 10
Afghanistan, 2–6, 10, 13, 18, 20, 43, 58, 66–67, 71, 72, 79, 81, 109
Afghan war, 43, 45, 54–56, 67, 68, 74, 75, 97, 114, 115
Ali Akbar Khan, Amir, 91
Ali Hussein, Sheik, 91, 111, 112
Ali Murad Khan, Amir, 57, 82, 83, 86–102 *passim*, 111, 112, 115
Ahmed, Syed, 33
Arthur, Sir George, 78, 97, 104, 116
Ashley, Lord, 109
Astall, William, 19–20
Auckland, Lord, 31–33, 35, 37, 38, 40–68 *passim*, 71, 109, 115

Bahawal Khan, 11, 26, 62, 73, 76, 80
Bahawalpur, 26, 60, 62, 73, 76, 83, 95, 96
Baluchistan, 72
Baluch tribes, viii, 39, 49–51, 82, 85, 90, 91, 99, 103, 104, 106. *See also* Kalhoras; Talpurs
Barclay, Lt. Col., 14, 15, 17
Barlow, Sir George, 4–5
Behram Khan, 34
Bell, Ross, 57, 58, 64
Bengal presidency, 110
Bentinck, William, Lord, 19, 21, 22, 25–28, 32, 45, 60, 118
Bhiria, 98
Bhung Bhara, 80

Bibarak Khan, Bugti, 72–80
Board of Control, vii, 18, 56, 68, 69, 104, 105, 107, 115
Bolan Pass, 47, 114
Bombay, 81, 111
Bombay presidency, 2, 3, 6, 9, 13–17, 30–32, 78, 97, 111
Brown, Lt. E. J., 57, 77–78, 87, 91, 93, 103, 111
Bukkur, 54, 55, 59, 73, 76, 79, 81
Burnes, Dr. James, *A Narrative of a Visit to the Court of Sinde*, 18–19, 113
Burnes, Sir Alexander, 21–22, 31–33, 38–39, 43–45, 54, 55, 63, 66, 67, 115
Bushire, 6, 9

Carless, Captain, 31, 32, 59
Carnac, Sir James, 32
Chandio Sardar, 81
Char Yar, 3, 13, 27, 39, 123 n
Clare, Lord, 22, 26
Clerk, Sir George, 72, 111
Clibborn, Maj. T., 77, 82, 85, 90, 91
Crow, Nathan, 2–5, 118
Cutch, 7, 8, 11–18 *passim*, 113; Run of, 15

Dalhousie, Lord, 111–112
Dhinji, 90, 91
Dost Mahomed Khan, 43, 44
Duncan, Jonathan, 2, 4, 7, 9, 10

INDEX

East India Company, vii, 1–11 *passim*, 14, 18–20, 61, 65, 68, 69, 73, 76, 109–120 *passim*; Secret Committee, 12, 18, 23, 28, 36–38, 41, 45, 56–58, 69, 104–106; General Court of Directors, 110; General Court of Proprietors, 110

Eastwick, E. B., *Dry Leaves from Young Egypt*, 78

Eastwick, W. J., 48, 49, 54, 60, 110, 118

Edmonstone, Neil B., 10

Ellenborough, Lord, 18, 19, 20, 68–90 *passim*, 92, 93, 96, 101, 104–117 *passim*

Elphinstone, Mountstuart, 15

Evans, Col. De Lacey, *On the Designs of Russia*, 18, 19

Fane, Sir Henry, 54

Fatehali Khan, Amir, viii, 2–4, 39. See also *Char Yar*

Fateh Ali Khan, Amir (the younger), 103

Fateh Ali Khan (Persian envoy), 7

Fateh Mahomed Ghori, 58, 72, 79, 82

Ferozepur, 59, 80, 116

Fitzgerald, Lord, 104, 105

Fort St. George presidency, 17

Fort William, 66

France, 1–8 *passim*, 113

Ganges River, 80, 113

Gholam Shah, 101

Ghulamali Khan, Amir, 3–12 *passim*, 123 n. See also *Char Yar*

Gladstone, William E., 106

Gordon, Brig. W., 58

Gough, Lord, 111

Grindley, Lt., 7

Hala, 100, 102

Harappa, viii

Hassal Ben Butcha, 54

Hathorn, Dr., 30, 31

Heddle, Dr. J. F., 30–32

Herat, 44, 47

Himalayas, 69

Hobhouse, Sir J. C. (Lord Broughton), 56–59, 63, 68, 115

Holmes, Col., 14

Hume, Joseph, 107, 110

Hussein Ali Khan, Amir, 64, 86, 93, 94, 98, 103

Hyderabad, viii, 2, 3, 7, 8, 11, 13, 23–27 *passim*, 39, 40, 49, 54, 56, 57, 60–65 *passim*, 72–76 *passim*, 86, 90, 94, 97–103 *passim*, 111, 113

Hyderabad, Amirs of, 14, 15, 22, 56, 60, 62, 63, 65, 71–72, 75, 81, 84, 85, 89, 93, 94, 98–103 *passim*; "treasonable" letters, 46, 76, 80, 99, 109, 117

Imamgarh, 90–92

Indus River, 5, 18, 30–37 *passim*, 42, 46, 50, 56, 60, 63, 67, 69, 71, 75, 79–81, 97, 106, 108, 111, 113, 119, 120; surveys of, 19–22, 30, 31; commerce on, 23, 26, 80, 113–114; tariffs, 24–27, 48, 49, 54, 59–62, 74, 75, 106, 114; Heddle's memoir, 31–32; steamer service, 32, 59, 79–81

Jacob, John, 98–101 *passim*, 104

Jaipur, 6

Jeth Anand, 60–62

Jhelum River, 36–37

Jocelyn, Lord, 109

Jodhpur, 6, 13; Rajah of, 11

Jokhias, Jam of, 81

Juswunt Rao Holkar, 12

Kabul, 3, 7, 9, 11, 18, 25, 33, 43, 44, 54, 67, 68

Kalhoras, viii, 106. *See also* Baluch tribes

Kandahar, 6, 7

Kanwar Naunihal Singh, 34

158

INDEX

Karachi, 2, 3, 11, 13, 50, 59, 60, 73–76, 79, 102, 117, 119; seized by British, 51–54
Karam Ali Khan, Amir, 123 n. See also *Char Yar*
Keane, Sir John, 38, 51
Kelat, 13, 58; Khan of, 72
Kennedy, Capt., 57
Khairpur, viii, 23–26, 30, 54–60 *passim*, 64, 66, 72, 78, 82–99 *passim*, 103, 112
Khairpur, Amirs of, 22, 62, 71–76, 81–85 *passim*, 89–103 *passim*; Turban, 82–83, 88–91, 93, 96, 112
Khera, P. N., *British Policy Toward Sindh up to the Annexation*, 36–37
Khiva, 18
Khosa tribe, 14, 17, 22, 23, 113
Khusru Beg, Mirza, 99
Khyber Pass, 5, 47
Khyeri tribe, 91
Khyer Mahomed, 54
Kot Diji, 89, 91, 112
Kukrala, 3
Kunhera, 98, 101

Lahore, 9, 18, 20, 22, 26, 34, 36, 40, 41, 72, 115
Lambrick, H. T., *Sir Charles Napier and Sind*, 72, 83, 87, 89, 92, 98, 103, 112, 118–119
Larkhana, 82, 85
Leckie, Lt., 21, 49, 50, 66
Lewis, George Cornwall, 120
Lower Sind. *See* Hyderabad
Luahiana, 26, 45
Luna (Cutch), 14

Mackeson, Lt., 38
Macnaghten, Sir William, 28, 31, 32, 35–48 *passim*, 52, 67
Macpherson, Maj., 78
Maddock, T. H., 73, 77
Mahmud of Ghazni, viii

Mahomed Ali Khan, Amir, 55
Mahomed Khan, Amir, 55, 90, 99
Mahomed Shah, 11
Mahomed Sharif, Syed, 72, 79
Maitland, Adm. Sir Frederick, 51, 54
Malcolm, Gen., 5
Mandavi, 7, 21
Manora, Fort of, 51, 54
Marathas, 1, 3
Marri tribe, 100, 101
Mazari tribe, 34, 36–38, 41
Melvill, Capt. P. M., 42
Metcalfe, Sir Charles, 14, 21, 26, 34, 119
Miani, vii, 101; battle of, 103–105, 115, 116
Mill, James, 120
Minto, Lord, 5–6, 9–10, 12
Mir Mahomed Khan, Amir, 53, 86, 98, 100, 103
Mirpur, viii, 51, 56, 103
Mithankot, 33, 34, 73
Mohiuddin (munshi), 87
Moira, Lord, 13, 16–18
Mubarak Khan, Amir, 24, 55, 56, 63, 66, 79, 112
Multan, 33, 34, 72
Murad Ali Khan, Amir, 18, 22–27, 39, 123 n. See also *Char Yar*
Muzaffer Khan, Kuwal, 8

Nadir Shah, viii
Napean, Sir Evan, 13
Napier, Com. Sir Charles, 109
Napier, Sir Charles, vii, 69–120 *passim*; biography, 70–71; as Governor of Sind, 106–107
Napier, William, 69, 78, 108, 120
Nara, 91, 98
Nasir Khan, Amir of Hyderabad, 41, 53, 59, 64, 72–76, 80–84, 86, 98–105 *passim*
Nasir Khan, Amir of Khairpur, 57, 63–66, 75, 76, 80, 81, 84, 99, 100, 102, 105

159

INDEX

Nathan, W. H., 31
Nehru, Jawaharlal, *Toward Freedom*, 118
Nott, Gen. Sir William, 58
Nur Mahomed, Amir, 27, 28, 30, 31, 37, 39–42, 46–50, 53, 54, 62, 64

Outram, James, 49, 57–62 *passim*, 65, 66, 72–74, 76, 81, 84, 91–104 *passim*, 108, 111, 114, 117, 119

Palmerston, Lord, 44, 68, 115
Parkur, 14, 39
Peel, Sir Robert, 105–106, 109–110, 117
Persia, 5–9, 18, 20, 43, 44, 46, 47, 79
Peshawar, 33, 43, 44
Petamber (munshi), 61
Postans, Capt. T., 64, 72
Pottinger, Henry, 11, 22–28 *passim*, 31, 35, 37–42 *passim*, 46–52 *passim*, 57, 60–64 *passim*, 115, 117
Prinsep, Henry, 23
Punjab, viii, 34

Rajput Sodhas, 13
Ranjit Singh, 20–26, 30, 34–47 *passim*; invades Sind, 32–38
Richardson, Mr., 77
Ripon, Lord, 105, 107–108
Roebuck, J. A., 109
Rohri, 54, 79–82, 85, 86, 112
Rojhan, 34, 35, 37
Rousseau, Joseph, 7
Russia, 1, 5, 8, 18, 19, 43, 44, 113, 114
Rustam Khan, Amir, 22–25, 38, 54–58, 63, 64, 72–94 *passim*, 96, 98, 99, 101, 104, 111, 112, 115, 117

Sabzalkot, 9, 73, 76, 80
Saddler, Capt., 17
Sanwanmal, Divan, 34–35, 72, 80
Scinde Irregular Horse, 98
Scindia, 6
Sehwan, 70
Seton, Capt. David, 7–9
Shahbunder, 3
Shahdad Khan, Amir, 65, 89, 98, 102
Shahdadpur, 104
Shahgarh, 91
Shah Shuja-ul-Mulk, 8, 11, 43–49, 52, 53, 56, 63–67 *passim*, 114
Shera, 101
Sher Mahomed Khan, Amir, 51, 56, 60–62, 103–104
Sher Singh, 72, 79, 117
Shikarpur, 13, 26, 30, 34–39, 46, 48, 52, 64–67, 73, 75, 76, 79, 85
Sikhs, 25, 34, 39–41, 43, 64, 72, 115
Simonitch, Count, 44
Sind-Baluchistan political department, 77, 81, 97–98
Smith, Nicholas Hankey, 6, 9–12, 51
Sobdar Khan, Amir, 39, 46, 50, 53, 61, 85, 86, 94, 98, 103, 114–115
Sohrab Khan, Amir, viii, 95
Soliman Shah, Syed, 67
Stanley, Lt., 85
Suffur Hubshee, 66
Sukkur, 57, 59, 73, 76–83 *passim*, 86, 96
Sultan Shahi, 33
Sutlej River, 36, 80

Talpurs, viii, 60, 73, 78, 82, 88–91, 94, 98, 106, 111, 112. *See also* Baluch tribes
Tatta, 3, 56, 59, 76, 93
Tharo Khan, Amir, viii
Thorton, A. P., *The Imperial Idea and Its Enemies*, 117

160

INDEX

Tipu Sultan of Mysore, 1
Treaties
 with Cutch: of 1816, 14; of 1819, 14
 with Hyderabad and Khairpur: of 1808, 8–9; of 1809, 11–12; of 1820, 17; of 1832, 23–25, 60, 66, 73, 114; of 1834, 28–29, 30, 60, 114; of 1838–39, 39–41, 49–50, 53–57, 60–63, 72, 74, 89, 114; of 1843, 74–102 *passim*
 with Lahore: of 1809, 34, 36; of 1838, 45–46
 with Mirpur: of 1841, 56
 of Nunahar, 57, 95, 111, 112
 Tripartite, 45–46
Trevelyan, C. E., 26

Umarkot, 8, 13

Upper Sind. *See* Khairpur

Valiant, Brig. T., 51, 54
Ventura, Gen., 23, 33
Vikovitch, Capt., 44

Wade, Col. Sir Claude, 35–43 *passim*
Wallace, Col., 85
Warden, Francis, 14–17
Wellesley, Lord, 2–5
Wellington, Duke of, 18, 78, 108, 116
William, Fort, 66
Williams, James, 17
Wood, Lt., 32

Zaman Shah, viii, 2–4, 8

CPSIA information can be obtained
at www.ICGtesting.com
Printed in the USA
JSHW030150280622
27538JS00001B/40